Can Do: A Seabee's Journey
Contributing Authors: Robert Amich and Catherine Boerner
Cover Design: Michael Nicloy
Interior Layout: Griffin Mill

All images have been provided by the authors.

ISBN: 979-8-9890505-8-1
Published by BC Books, LLC, Franklin, Wisconsin
Publisher: Brenda E. Cortez

BC
Books

Quantity order requests may be emailed to the Publisher:
info@bcbooksllc.com
Printed in The United States of America

CAN DO

A SEABEE'S JOURNEY

Compiled from the diary of Robert G. Behee

By Robert Amich and Catherine Boerner

This book is dedicated to the proud and brave Navy Seabees who fought hard and built the path to victory in World War II.

TABLE OF CONTENTS

INTRODUCTION

Throughout our childhood, our grandparents, whom we called Nana and Pawpaw, shared stories from their lives. Most stories were about their time in the Ringling Bros. and Barnum & Bailey Circus where they met. Very few stories were about their experiences during World War II. Our Pawpaw held these stories close to his heart. Out of respect, we didn't push. Luckily, he documented the experiences of his journey through the upheaval of World War II in his personal diary. This record reached its crescendo on the beaches of Normandy and continued to the South Pacific.

Standing on the precipice of a new era, we feel compelled to share our Pawpaw's story with the world. His diary is more than just a chronicle of experiences; it is a testament to the enduring legacy of those who came before us. It reminds us that freedom is not free but must be fought for and defended with every fiber of our being.

We invite you to journey with us through pages of history, following in the footsteps of a generation who faced the darkness of tyranny and emerged into the light of liberty. In our Pawpaw's words, we find not only the courage to face our challenges but also the hope that even in our darkest hour, the human spirit will always prevail.

~ Robert Amich and Catherine Boerner
Robert "Bob" Behee's only grandchildren

FOREWORD

By Andrew Boerner

"Thank you for your service." This statement is spoken so commonly today to any United States Armed Forces member that it may lose its emotional significance. It is nice that people feel compelled to thank someone who has served in the armed forces, but do they stop to understand what service means?

The details behind a veteran's service matter, but they are rarely heard by the outside world. One reason is that people under fire in the middle of combat are more concerned with survival and defeating the enemy than scribbling details into a journal for future readers. Historians are left trying to figure out what happened in the past by piecing together multiple first-person accounts to make sense of different events. It is not expected to have access to a soldier's daily feelings and experiences when heading to war or in the heat of battle.

Robert "Bob" Behee's diary is a rare gem, a unique window into the life of a soldier before, during, and after one of the most pivotal battles of World War II, the Invasion of Normandy, also known as D-Day. It's not just a record of events but a personal narrative that unveils the man behind the uniform. His courage, humor, hopes, and dreams, as well as his petty grievances and prejudices, all come to life in his own words.

I never had the privilege to speak with Bob Behee face-to-face. While the Nazis and the Imperial Japanese Army could not kill him, he died at age 74 from cancer on September 27th, 1991. This was two years before I met his granddaughter, Cathy, who became my wife. The first time I read Bob

Behee's diary, I thought, wow, what an incredible account of the World War II era. My gut told me others would be captivated by a firsthand glimpse into what it was like to be a Navy Seabee. I wanted to help make that happen.

After delving into Bob's experiences in WWII, you will gain a profound understanding of the physical, mental, and emotional sacrifices our veterans endured during the war. This newfound understanding will transform the way you perceive their service. The next time you express gratitude to a veteran, it may carry a deeper, more heartfelt meaning.

Editor's note: The following pages are Robert G. Behee's words with minimal syntax and spelling corrections to increase the level of authenticity. They contain some slang terms and ethnic slurs that would have been common during the 1940s.

CHAPTER

ONE

PRE-INVASION PREPARATION

This is being copied from the diaries I kept while in the service of my country. Before starting, I might say that I joined the Seabees on the 18th day of June 1943. I sailed for England on the 30th of January, 1944. I landed in Liverpool on February 12th. After Journeying to Falmouth, we were formed into groups and went on amphibious maneuvers. The first entry in my diary was made while I was aboard a ship off of South Wales. It should be noted that I was very angry during this time from March to April 1944.

March 10, 1944: Aboard the L.S.T. #72 [*Landing Ship Tank*]. The officers are getting steak and chicken for each meal. I heard they bought whiskey for $1.65 a quart and then sold 3 quarts to an enlisted man for $40.00. The officers are also selling a pack of cigarettes for $0.85 when the Navy price is $0.50. Enlisted men are fed cheap C-Rations and have to pay $1.05 for a pack of cards. Prices are up, and yet the canteen shows no profit. The officers foreflush meals for guests. Someone is getting wealthy on this ship. We were towed to Swansea, South Wales.

March 14, 1944: Aboard L.S.T. #389. Officers ate the same chow as enlisted men. They also ate last. We are the first crew in history to be towed on a Rhino [*a Tug and barge made up of pontoons that are connected and equipped with outboard engines, used to transport heavy equipment and people in shallow water*]

March 25, 1944: I found out that the man who distributes our rations to ships sells anything he can find to civilians to make a profit. Even our complimentary cigarettes.

April 1, 1944: Boarded L.S.T. #369. This is the heaviest armed L.S.T. that I have ever been on. It has ten 20mm cannons forward from the bridge. Jerries were over last night. Maybe this is it!!

April 2, 1944: We are getting the scraps from all the other ships. Other crews eat first, get ice cream, pie, etc. We get none. We fight harder-get slop. Same Navy, same war. Why??

April 4, 1944: Here is the difference between a Rhino Tug and a Rhino Barge. The Tug is powered by the two outboard Chrysler Marine motors and can hold 50 tons. The barge has two inboard Chrysler Marine motors and can hold 300 tons. Together, some are calling this our secret weapon for the invasion.

April 6, 1944: Returned to Swansea from three continuous days of operations. Largest practice landing yet. We went to two beaches. We had to Tug a wreck, but the L.S.T. refused to give us an extra boat. Still treated like dogs.

April 7, 1944: No sooner did we leave the ship than the officers made ice cream or some other delicacy.

April 28, 1944: Docked at Milford Haven, South Wales, 350 of 3,500 17- and 18-year-old "new boots" arrived here. These scared children have only been in the service for two months. They had been shipped over without training and apparently without all their shots.

There were some deaths as they crossed the "pond" [*Atlantic Ocean*], and now they are quarantined because of Scarlet Fever.

May 5, 1944: Sailing is delayed. A gale-force wind has been blowing for a week.

Apparently, this is delaying the invasion. I expect all of my crew to become casualties in the invasion.

May 6, 1944: Every one of us has seen the pontoons in action, which gives us little hope for survival. Even our ensign expects us to be butchered. It isn't funny anymore. The day is slowly drawing near. I expect it will come in June.

May 9, 1944: L.S.T. #5 is an excellent ship and crew. We spent our time in Milford Haven clearing out a cemetery and constructing autopsy boards and embalming tables. This town is turning into a big hospital base. It is being manned to accommodate thousands of future casualties.

May 12, 1944: We were issued new gas masks and other sorts of chemically treated equipment and clothing. We are going to leave all our other gear in Plymouth, England.

We will only take the bare necessities with us to France, along with our battle gear. I feel this is the beginning of the end. We will have lots of bullets and shells to go with us.

<u>May 15, 1944</u>: Our orders have changed. Our vessels are the heavily armored Rhino secret weapon. We are ordered to leave all money but 10 shillings. The admiral is said to be coming tomorrow. The Rhino Tug is nothing but a floating gas tank. A hit in it anyplace, and we are through.

<u>May 19, 1944</u>: I believe I am beginning to understand what is wrong with me and why I have so much I dislike in my common soldier. In conversations, I seem to know exactly what will be said next, and it most often is childish, uninteresting, and trite. Then again, it must be considered that my way of life is so unlike all of those I come into contact with. Their attempts at conversation are always the child of a sordid hearsay, immoral fallacy type. See, I still don't know how to express it.

[*Bob was 27 in 1944, quite a bit older than his fellow sailors*].

<u>May 20, 1944</u>: We were attacked as we were towing our new vessels to Portland Harbor, England. At 9:00, we began firing at a

12

ship off our starboard [*right*] side. It was over in three minutes, and we only had the fantail shot up. The E-Boats have been coming pretty close off the English coast. Two L.S.T.s plus crew and soldiers were lost last week. All the invasion forces are slowly pulling into position. There have been slight conflicts reported daily. Jerry planes have been flying over daily, taking a look at what we are doing.

May 21, 1944: Motored back to Plymouth and am astounded. The road to Plymouth, for what seems like 100 miles, is lined with trucks, jeeps, tanks, guns, ammo, and thousands of cans of fuel. All are ready to be loaded on the ships to head to France.

May 22, 1944: Moved with all of my battle gear to L.S.T. #314. This is to be my invasion ship.

May 24, 1944: A Jerry plane was shot down over the crowded harbor yesterday. Four mines were discovered and destroyed in the channel. Any hour now, we will load the ships with troops, and the battle of all battles will be on. I don't look for it until May 30th at the earliest. We are all going in with gas-protective clothes, eye shields, etc. Three layers of clothing will be worn, as gas is expected to repel our attack. We are planning to go to the beach in the second wave. The easiest way to remember my unit is to remember the number 1. I am in the 1st Platoon, vanguard (I) company, in the 111th Battalion, Tug #1, Rhino #1, 11th Amphibian Force. We are the first ship of the flotilla and the first scheduled to hit the beach in the second wave. Though hopefully we will not be the first to get hit.

May 25, 1944: King George was here today to look the invasion force over. On each British ship he boarded, the crew was given an extra tot of rum. Each American ship that he boarded was rewarded with a dish of ice cream!

The harbor is a very impressive sight, with landing craft of all descriptions as far as you can see. We still haven't taken any soldiers aboard, so D-Day must still be a few days off. All the L.S.T.s have been given rations and blankets for the G.I. Joes that will be joining us. We estimate that about 50 corpsmen will be on each vessel, along with 400 stretchers. The foot of my bunk is against bulkhead #13. Lucky for me, I am not superstitious. Machine guns are being mounted on the Rhino and the Tug. I watch L.C.T.s getting loaded with tanks, then moving out so that more ships can get loaded. If we put all of these ships together, it really would make a bridge to the continent. I figure that there are no less than 2,000 ships getting ready to go to war.

I got another shot today to try to prepare my body for the expected gas attack. I have been issued medicine, salves, pastes, and guards for the eyes, feet, and hands. I have so much gear that I am not sure if I will know what to grab first.

I have only the vaguest realization of the deaths and killings to come. I am still not scared or nervous. When enemy planes come over, I am only mildly interested. I do find myself hoping, so very hard, that I come through alive. Only two men out of the 36 of us are showing obvious fear. As H-Hour draws nearer, I'll make some notes about my mate's reactions. That is unless I myself am not scared so badly that I can't write.

There was no enemy action over Portland Harbor today. If this invasion works the first time and takes hold, I still may get home for Christmas. We are getting better and larger servings of chow lately.

May 26, 1944: King George and the Admirals left the ship today. We have nice, clean army clothes. "To be worn on French soil," our commander says. I guess we are going in as the army. I will never understand the United States military. D-Day still appears to be days off. Some have guessed that we might not leave for three weeks. Lord, I hope not! I'm anxious to the point of being irritable. Let's go! It looks like our landing will be made directly across the channel.

When we embark for H-Hour, I will place this tablet in an envelope, seal it, and send it to Mickey [*Bob's wife*]. I have another scratch pad that I will take with me for battle details.

May 28, 1944: Well, tonight, I had my baptism by fire, and things are still popping. Jerry flew over at 1:30 AM in force. The alarm went off after the first bombs dropped, and the shore batteries lit up the sky. The location of my bunk isn't the best. I'm in the bow, under the 40mm cannon, which really shakes things up. The only thing that is nearer to the front of the ship than I am is the ammunition room, which isn't good. I didn't get up for the run, but I did put on my helmet and stayed in my bunk. An all-clear was sounded about 30 minutes after the initial firing.

However, just as the gunners were crawling back into their bunks, all hell broke loose again. Jerry flares lit up the harbor. Two near misses nearly knocked me out of my bunk, so I got up and stood out on the main deck. Our planes went up during the Jerries second run, and it seemed like thousands of guns were firing on them. The barrage balloons were a marvelous thing during the attack. They forced Jerry to fly high and made their attacks far less accurate. We were able to shoot down at least one of their planes.

I realized during the raid how easily and quickly my insignificant life could be snuffed out. My hands sweated, and I was trembling. It was cold, and I was naked, so I honestly don't know if I was shaking from fear or the cold. Another fellow needed help calming down, so doing that job also calmed my nerves. When I looked around, the searchlights, flares, tracers, and explosions of all colors made a morbid yet beautiful sight.

Sailors thought it was strange that the Jerries did not drop many bombs in the second raid. This was explained in the morning at about 6:30 AM when the delayed mines that they did drop in the harbor began going off. Naturally, this got everyone to run to their battle stations again, even though there were no planes. I did see a mine blow up under a Higgins boat. The geyser looked like it was at least 200 feet high. When the water settled, only a few feet of the bow was visible. Three men were killed when the mine exploded under that small boat. The mines are still exploding, but it seems that no large ship was hit. We did find some slugs and shrapnel on the deck of the Rhino. All traffic in the harbor has been stopped until the minesweepers have finished their work.

At about 7:00 PM, hundreds of destroyers and warships with more firepower were brought into the harbor close to us. If Jerry attacks again, they will have a large audience tonight.

May 29, 1944: Another hectic night. After a few false starts, Jerry came over in force again at 1:00 AM. After they dropped a few bombs, we laid down a smoke screen, and they flew away. I believe I would rather face enemy fire than all of that smoke. I gagged and choked all night. I tried everything, even my gas mask, but still, I suffered. At least no more planes were blasting away at us. I was able to hear a sea battle being fought in the distance. All night long, more ships crammed into the harbor. I saw L.S.T.s, L.C.T.s, P.T.s, L.C.A.s, other troop ships, and light cruisers all poised to sail across the channel. We catch ourselves saying, "If we live through the night." It is so close we can feel it.

May 30, 1944: The entire ship's crew is restricted. Army advance boarded this AM. The rest of the troop is due tomorrow. I cruised outside the nets this morning and noticed 75-80 big warships out there. It is only a matter of days. My guess is Sunday, June 4th. One of the crazy sailors had a sign made that said, "The SeaBees have landed, Battalion 111." Our crew is to put it on the beach when we land.

It is going to be a bloody mess Statistically, we are set to lose over 50% of our men on the initial landing. Everyone feels deep down that he will stay alive. My knowledge of this leads me to wonder how everyone is going to do when the going gets rough. Or, if Jerry doesn't have a surprise that will knock us all back into the sea. Trouble is expected tonight; wish me luck.

May 31, 1944: Thankfully, it was a quiet night. As I write this, our L.S.T. is loading with troops and equipment. Everyone is really talkative and nervous as we make our final preparations. We have a dog named "Sad Sack" who is going on the invasion with us.

I'd like to take her home with me if I pull through. There is fog today, but the L.S.T.s and L.C.T.s are loading rapidly. I think we will have everything loaded within the next day or two.

June 1, 1944: All loaded and standing by. The loading of the other crafts is going on a 24-hour basis. The soldiers have brought a phonograph with them. The music is very tantalizing. However, since the army came aboard, our chow has fallen away to nothing. Just Spam and other canned foods. The fog kept Jerry away. I hope he stays away tonight. We now have, amongst all the supplies, 90 tons of TNT. One hit and I will be waking up at the "pearly gates."

June 2, 1944: Tomorrow morning, we are to take our sea bags and all our belongings onto the Rhino Tug. Once we board it, we are not to leave it until we reach the French coast. Rumor has it we will be landing on a half dozen different spots, which is most likely true. We will get additional news at the briefing tonight. It is now probably a matter of hours before we leave.

At the briefing, I discovered we are now in the First Wave. The first 10 Rhinos will be cut loose 10 miles from the enemy. Later, Waves will be towed closer to the beach. Two battleships and ten destroyers will lay a fierce barrage on the shore batteries. The waters are expected to be heavily mined the closer we get to the beach. It's going to be terrible. The Rangers will be the first ashore. H-Hour is planned to be 4:00 AM. My crew is to hit the beach at H-Hour plus 40 minutes. I'm scared of those mines. The entire coast is probably teaming with TNT. The enemy is firmly encased in the cliffs over the beach. There are 4-5 thicknesses of mines and blockades. The code name given to the short beach we will be landing on is called "Omaha." There are 15 machine gun pillboxes located on that beach.

Odds are 1 in 4 that poison gas will be used to stop us. I'm sealing this diary now, and so help me; one day, I will unseal it again.

June 3, 1944: I have put on my long underwear and impregnated clothing. We are now outside of the harbor, lined up in convoy formation. Naturally, we are first. There are easily a couple of hundred ships around me.

We leave early in the morning at about 5 knots (5.7 mph). The first soldiers are set to step foot in France at 4:00 AM on Monday,

June 5th. I am aboard this Tugboat, and I am not supposed to leave it until the landings have been completed and the enemy has been completely pushed back. No more hot food until "who knows when." I am wearing my gas-repellent gear, but I hope I won't need it. No hope of any relief or reinforcements for two weeks. No washing, shaving, toilet or beds.

CHAPTER
TWO

INVASION

<u>June 4, 1944</u>: We are finally underway. It is 2:30 AM, everybody is asleep, and I am standing watch. At 9:00 AM, we turned around and headed back to England. We are right back where we started. This could be for a number of reasons. I'm inclined to believe that it was a false start to confuse the enemy. All the ships are in their same positions, outside of the nets. We will probably head back out into the channel again in a few hours. Sleeping on the cold steel is misery. I guess the only thing you can do is go without sleep for a few days so that, eventually, you will be able to sleep anywhere.

My emotions are still reigned in. I had a tight feeling in my chest yesterday for a while. Today, it seems far away, sort of unreal. I can visualize what's to come, but not well enough to have actual fear. We've all seen too many movies, I guess. It does give one a strange feeling sitting here on a small Tug bobbing in the English Channel. The experience really gets your senses going. I hear the Tug booming and clanking. I feel the wind and waves trying to get at my skin. I look around me and see numerous ships, all loaded to the hilt with men, equipment, and guns everywhere. Then I remember this harbor only holds a small fraction of the total invasion force. What a mighty force we have put together to take on the Nazis.

At 7:00 PM, we have a meeting. We are told the mission last night was intended to draw the German E-Boats out so they would not get in the way during the actual invasion. So now I am waiting as the rain begins and the waters become choppier.

June 5, 1944: At 2:00 AM, we are underway again. We are headed down the coast, and our convoy is at least 5 miles long. Our planes fly around us in pairs. We have not seen the enemy yet, but we are ready. At 2:00 PM, we are joined by another convoy of destroyers with more planes flying overhead. Someone on our Tug found an American flag. It flies only a few feet above my head when I am behind the helm (it occasionally hits me in the head). However, it is nice to have a wee bit of America as we sit bobbing in the English Channel like a cork. We had no enemy action as we headed East for the first 10 hours; now that we are heading South East, we have not seen the enemy, but we have seen Spitfires and P-38 Lightnings flying over us in steadily increasing numbers. Another convoy of destroyers joined up with us and then suddenly changed direction.

June 6, 1944: It is 1:00 AM, and it is cold as hell. Everyone is soaked. There are eight of us on the Rhino Tug. Of the eight, five have seasickness. I am one of the fortunate three, and I am currently standing watch now. Orders are all hands-on deck at 3:00 AM, with helmets, masks, and guns ready for action. It's 4:30 AM, and the battle is on.

This was the time we were supposed to hit the beach, but that is not ready to happen. We had a little engine trouble, but I was able to get things back on track as we were able to take more men aboard. I have no fear now. We have yet to run the minefields. The firing from the Germans on the French coast looks like a colorful 4th of July from this distance. I have to remind myself that as long as the Germans are firing, we are not able to approach the beach.

It's 12:00 PM, and we have been laying off the minefield for hours. The enemy still holds the beach. We are the boss of the sky so far, but it doesn't seem to matter much. I am so tired. I have been up since 1:00 AM, and I haven't changed my clothes since June 2nd.

It's 7:00 PM, and the Germans are still shooting. The big German guns have made a wreck of everything we have put ashore. Beach One is one huge cloud of smoke from the numerous fires that their artillery started.

We are still floating offshore. We started to move in once, but enemy fire drove us back. I have witnessed several direct hits on L.C.T.s with heavy casualties. The beach is littered with our craft. Our ships are still shelling the cliffs.

At 11:30 PM, we were still laying 1,000 yards off the coast, waiting for the guns to be knocked out. At that time, several Jerry planes flew over us, dropping mines and bombs. One plane flew about 100 feet over our Tug. During the first attack, which lasted about an hour, we cruised around, trying to take evasive maneuvers. I saw two planes get shot down in flames. One landed about 300 feet from us. We towed a boat with wounded aboard who was stuck on the beach. We tied up to a larger ship at 2:00 AM to examine the

Tug. It had taken an awful beating and was starting to slowly come apart. We did some quick patchwork and headed off again.

June 7, 1944: It's raining again. Jerry came back again at 5:00 AM. They focused on the bigger ships. The shore batteries are still dueling with the ships now. It was murder yesterday, but we are about a day behind where we were supposed to be. We have to get in today because there are 50 L.S.T.s that are waiting for us to unload them.

At 9:00 AM, we are being shelled because we have moved our Tug 1,000 feet from the shore. I discovered that I did not remember much from the second air raid last night because, somehow, I had slept through it. When I awoke, my head was sore from beating it against metal pontoons for hours. I must have been beyond tired, and after being up for 25 hours without sitting down, my body just said, "Enough."

It is hard for me to understand why we are not on the beach yet. We have hundreds of ships laying off the coast. Our planes fly up and down the beach practically unmolested. There are some soldiers who have established a beachhead. Yet, our ships are still shelling the coast, and they are still firing back at our ships (There were seve n near misses just now on a battleship). The men before us have gone in, yet we stand by. There are some very lovely cliffs for the enemy to lodge in and escape our bombs and shells. Omaha Beach still looks very formidable. I have no fear yet. We've all been wet since it began. My feet are freezing. It is very windy now, and that is making the water quite rough. As each new event takes place, I think I must jot it down so I can read it later. See, I do believe I will live through this.

CHAPTER
THREE

OMAHA BEACH

At 10:00 AM, on June 7th, we finally started for the beach. At 11:50 AM, we touched France for the first time. Bodies litter the beach and the immediate surf. A few shells are still exploding around us. Many troops are now landing along with tanks and heavy guns. The Germans have been pushed back from the beach. We took four heavily wounded soldiers back with us to the L.S.T. One man had his arm blown off.

At 2:00 PM, we began unloading L.S.T. #334. It had to be unloaded in two loads. The Germans are now reported to be 8-25 miles away from the beach. Our big guns are firing way inland. I guess it is safe to say that the beachhead is firmly established. One section of the beach is still mined, but I believe the most-bloody part is over for me. Now, all that remains is the hard work. To make matters worse, I have a dandy cold and am still wet.

We are bringing a lot of young soldiers to the beach. When they leave the larger ships, they act all cocky and say things like, "How is it going over there?" as they laughingly point at the beach. As we get closer and they see all of the dead bodies, they become quieter and more serious. In addition to all of the bodies, there are many sunken craft there as well.

I have seen the waves washing over many small boats, L.C.T.s, L.C.Is, and L.C.V.P.s that didn't make it off the beach. Our planes continue to fly around the beach in formations of 16s and 20s with apparently no losses.

At 4:00 PM, I watch from the beach as demolition squads blow up mines. They are able to see all of the obstacles that the

Germans placed in the water much better at low tide. However, some men are still being lost as the mines are exploded.

It has stopped raining and is turning into a beautiful day. There are ships as far as the eye can see in any direction. There is still some occasional fire from the hills. One shot "tinged" uncomfortably close to me. There must still be some snipers who were bypassed by our troops.

At 6:00 PM, I have my Rhino high and dry on the beach. Yesterday, at this time, it would have been certain death to do this as the Jerries were still in a position to shell any beached craft. The infantry soldiers had to get out in water waist-deep and wade a quarter of a mile down the beach to miss the mined area. The Rhino is still loaded with vehicles because it is not yet safe to bring it fully loaded through the mined waters. I am still constantly hearing mines going off. The Tug still has a line on the Rhino idling 400 feet offshore. There were literally thousands of mines the Germans laid on this beach that our Tug can float over, but the heavier ships cannot.

A bomber knocked out a German machine gun nest in the hills about an hour ago, and they just refused to quit. We can hear the battle still raging in the distance. Somehow, I envy the assault troops. They get to keep moving on. I heard a rumor that of the six beach landings, ours was the final beachhead to be established. We're set now. There are barrage balloons over the ships by the score to keep Jerry away. If balloons will win the war, sell your war bonds now! We are only a few minutes flying time from the Jerry landing fields. So, he will most likely be visiting us often (only at night, the coward). We've been on the job for 39 hours. That's 39 hours of war. We finally left for France 65 hours ago. However, I boarded the Tug 137 hours ago.

June 8, 1944: We were able to complete
the landing at 10:00 PM. From 8:00 PM until
about 9:30 PM, we were being shelled by
German artillery. What I was doing was hard
work, but it was made even more difficult
when you have to take cover when a shell
flies over your head. Lucky for us they all
missed their target. We were finally relieved
at 11:00 PM. Then we drove around in an
L.C.M. until about 3:30 AM looking for the
Wheelock [*a ship he was supposed to dock
with*]. Jerry planes were over in force as we
were looking for the "missing" ship. They
bombed some of the ships, but they missed
us. I was bitterly cold and wet. Since we
could not find the ship, we found a damaged
L.C.T. on the beach, and I slept until 7:00
AM. When it was light, we went off in search
of the Wheelock again and found it only a
quarter of a mile from our starting point. It
sure would be nice to be able to see in the
dark. When we went aboard, I could see
that the ship was overcrowded with no extra

beds, but they did have a hot meal for us. An observation: since we left England, I have only seen three Limey ships and no Limey troops.

CHAPTER
FOUR

REFLECTION TIME

Now that I have some time to sit, I can remember some of the gory happenings I have seen over the past two days that it's best to try and forget. I wish I can write home and tell everyone that I am alright instead of just recording it in this diary. Not even as much as a "pain in my sawdust," as Mickey would say. [*This is a reference to the words of a popular song at the time. When you know something is wrong with you, but you can't tell people the details*]. I am just very, very weary. By 9:30 AM, the ship is crowded to the hilt, with all divisions of troops resting and seeking relief. With so many men around, the scuttlebutt flies thick and fast. It is hard to tell what is true and what is the figment of a joker's imagination. One of the men said he had heard of the Germans using poison gas. Someone else said they saw German soldiers on the beach wearing American uniforms and waving the troops in to slaughter them. A signalman backed up this story by saying he flagged ashore for permission to land. At first, he did not get an answering signal. Then he said that a man from the hill waved him in.

A short while later, the artillery was turned loose on him, and it was havoc. He said he saw a man take a direct hit by a shell, and the only thing left was his boots with his feet still in them. I hope this story is not true because it would be hard to trust anyone you see as we approach a beach.

I heard an international broadcast and there was not much mention about the U.S. forces. I think it is clear that our landing was the hardest and the costliest. The hills here are honeycombed with tunnels, ala Cassino. Jerry still holds part of the hill. One machine gun pillbox killed 400 American soldiers before a battleship took it out. Of the 60 L.C.M.s that took place in the First Wave, only 15 pulled away from the beach [*We have not verified if Bob's assertions were factual*]. The radio said that the first landings began at 7:15 AM. This was not true because I saw the first wave hit the beach around 4:00 AM. I'm beginning to realize how fortunate I was that our advance to the beach was halted by the beachmaster and German fire. If we had continued at 5:00 AM as we intended, we would have been shelled into oblivion.

Some men from the 111th Battalion are still on the beach, and more ships keep dropping off more men. Our commander said he wants the 111th Battalion to be a strictly amphibious force. No construction, just landing and combat. I hope this means after we get everything mopped up over here, I will get sent home without worrying about being sent to the South Pacific. A man can dream. We have been informed that the entire

111th Battalion is set to start living ashore in three days. We will look more like army soldiers because we will be living in pup tents and foxholes.

The radio said that Germany is upset with our successful invasion. They said Rommel is set to lead a huge counterattack soon. Hitler is quoted as saying, "I don't expect to stop a landing, but we can certainly push them back into the sea." We are still holding our breaths out of fear of retaliation.

The bombers just left to return to England. This means that darkness will soon fall, and the Jerries will be back for a visit. None of our planes are over here after dark. So, we shoot at any plane we see until morning. I would rather be out in the open, on my Tug during an attack. I feel that it is safer. Most of the Tugs have been wrecked. Rhino #4 and #7 hit mines. We have been very, very lucky so far. Rumor has it we are to make another landing farther up the coast in a couple of weeks. If this is true, we should probably have this beach secured completely. It is clear to me that Jerry knew we were going to hit this particular beach. Our big guns were firing all day inland.

CHAPTER

FIVE

AIR RAID

June 9, 1944: We endured a tremendous air raid last night. The planes strafed the Rhino and Tug at 11:00 PM. The Rhino is a wreck and there is only one motor left on the Tug after it was hit. It seems to me that all of the Rhinos are wrecked and need repairs. Three Liberty Ships have been purposely scuttled 500 feet from the shore to act as a breakwater. We are now tied up beside them, facing the beach as I watch the L.S.T.s hit the beach. At 7:00 PM, we moved aboard one of the scuttled ships (The Potter) to try and get some sleep. More ships continue to stream into the area, but because of all the wrecks, they run a higher chance of hitting something in this huge battleground of ships. Firing is still close enough to cause this sunken hull to tremble. Incidentally, the water is just deep enough at high tide to cover the main deck.

This means we have to sleep on the deck of the officer's quarters while they get to sleep inside on beds. Even now, the officers still get 1000% more and better than enlisted sailors. We have been told there are still snipers in the hills and that we need to get our guns in good working shape. I hope we can finish unloading all of these boats soon so I can get into the scrap. I hate just being a target.

At 9:15 PM, the German planes came back. We have been warned that a big German counter attack is expected for today or tomorrow. Orders came a short while ago to rush badly needed big guns to shore to repel the Germans. I fear we have not seen the most vigorous enemy action yet. The latest scuttlebutt is that the snipers are not

Germans but are French women who don't like Americans. I hope this rumor is not true.

<u>June 10, 1944</u>: We did not come through the last air raid unscathed. It seemed that Jerry attacked us all night long. When the sun came up, I could see there were quite a few casualties on my ship. The army had rounded up some German prisoners who seemed to be composed of kids and older men. I don't speak German well, but it seemed to me these men and boys did not enjoy being captured.

They were even more upset when they were put to work digging graves for the American boys their countrymen had killed. Rhino #17 was hit hard last night. Of the 80 soldiers on it, nine were killed.

I found out more information about what our boys faced when the First Wave hit the beaches. The German machine gunners waited until the landing craft let down their ramps until they unloaded thousands of bullets to cut down our men. I think the mines were more merciful because the person was blown to bits in most instances and did not have to suffer.

June 11, 1944: The Jerries were over for the longest period yet. They first hit us at 11:30 PM and they have been with us way past daybreak. The First Wave only had eleven planes, but they headed right for us and the merchant ships. It got plenty hot out here. I haven't heard the reports on casualties yet. I still see and hear mines going off occasionally. A "Duck" was blown up yesterday by a mine while heading to the beach. This shows that there are still dangerous underwater mines.

I have heard a rumor that the Germans were using a wooden bullet for close range that splinters when it enters the body, causing maximum damage. I hope this is not true. I just saw a bomb hit about 100 yards away from me.

At about 8:00 PM, the big guns seemed to have fallen silent. It is my hope that the enemy has been pushed out of their range.

That would mean it is less likely the Germans will be able to counterattack soon. However, we are still preparing. Many more troops have landed on the beach today.

The situation is not so good aboard my scuttled home. Fresh water is running short and we have little for drinking and cooking. Food is going bad because there are ice boxes that are not working. The plumbing is also out.

June 12, 1944: First quiet night in an age. As far as I know, only one observation plane appeared at dusk. Something must be up. The mere lack of fighting disturbed our sleep.

We are all lying in wait for the drone of the plane propellers, heralding the beginning of an attack. Oddly enough, I discovered that most of us sleep through the raids. Three of the nine men sleeping in my room always stumble to the deck after the first shot. Poor judgment; those guys are never going to get any sleep. At 7:00 PM, General Eisenhower is coming to the cliffs to look things over.

Troops have been landing around the clock. I have even seen more Limey boats around here.

CHAPTER
SIX

LIVING IN
A FOXHOLE

June 13, 1944: German bombers really gave it to the beachhead. Heavy bomb flashes were visible continuously from about 11:30 PM until 4:00 AM. When it was light, we could see the damage to the beach was relatively slight. Rumor has it that Jerry is putting all of his available planes into one squadron and is bombing one beach per night. When it comes back to our beach again, I tremble at the thought. There are lots of mines and TNT going off this morning. It seems the demolition squads are blowing up the wrecks so that we can get more supplies to the shore.

The beach has been mostly cleared of the dead bodies and wrecks. The wooded area around the beach still stinks of death. Many booby traps are still uncleared.

We have been only eating two meals a day. Most of the stores are underwater most of the time. Now I understand why we were given so many shots before we left. Our living conditions are mostly unsanitary.

There is still more talk about another invasion soon. The enemy has been pushed back 27 miles. This means we are 1/50th the distance to victory. Yet, we still think that a German counter-offensive is still possible.

At 6:00 PM, our forces are at the German's second line of defense. It seems to us we are fighting young kids. Although the thought is that Rommel and his Panzers will roll in soon. It seems like Hitler is sacrificing these inferior troops as a delaying tactic.

He might be onto something. There are not many tanks supporting the American troops.

Of the 60 tanks in one division, only eight made it off the beach. It seems to me that our troops are advancing too fast to complete mop-up duties properly. One example is all of the snipers they have left behind. Heavy American casualties are the result. One sniper surrendered on a hill today. He said, "The only reason I came out of hiding was that I have no food. You would never have found me." He would have been found eventually, but not before he had taken more American lives.

British troops on the next beach reported a trap yesterday. Our troops successfully were able to go to their rescue. The impending drive by the Nazis will determine our next move. If it looks as if this beach will not hold, we will make another landing on a beach behind their lines. We have captured 1,500 German prisoners from the front. Orders are, no more prisoners from behind front lines.

We are getting low on supplies, including ammunition. Our ship is almost out of shells.

The one behind us is out altogether.

June 14, 1944: A comparatively quiet night last night. Our infantry was forced to use captured German guns and ammunition because of the heavy loss of equipment on the landing. This, along with supply ships delaying in being offloaded, has led to a general shortage in ammunition. All of the ships in the harbor have been ordered not to fire until the planes are within 1000 yards as a way to save ammunition. L.S.T #314 was rumored to have been sunk after we left her. Apparently, this is true because she is way overdue on her return trip. The Seabees blew up several mines ashore today.

At 7:00 PM, I set up my pup tent shelter on top of the cliff. This is not the safest area because there are still mines here. The mines that have not been found yet are enclosed in wooden boxes, so the mine detectors don't find them. My helmet is lying in a hole that was left when a mine was dug up.

I had my first mail call while on French soil. Some French boys stopped by us on the beach today. One of them remarked to an infantry soldier, "Got any gum, chum?" This produced a roar of laughter from soldiers around him. I think I did see one of the soldiers give him a stick for his courage. Not as many ships are left in the harbor. Probably around 200. At 11:00 PM, enemy planes flew over us as I lay on the cold ground under a flimsy canvas. Luckily, they were not interested in me.

June 15, 1944: Jerry attacked all night. Anti-aircraft guns seemed to erupt all around me. We were kept awake all night, or we were awake half a dozen times. This afternoon, two men were blown up while removing mines from our campsite. Five hundred mines have been removed from the field, and they discover more by the hour. A new cement block type of mine is now being discovered. A mine detector is worthless in this case.

They are painted green and laid in the grass, where they are well camouflaged. I spent the morning digging in, and now I have a foxhole under my pup tent. I slept through the biggest part of the raid last night. In the morning, I found a hole in my tent and a piece of shrapnel next to me for a "pillow." When I went outside, I found an unexploded 25mm shell by my doorstep. So, I guess the fighting was closer than I thought.

CHAPTER
SEVEN

NAZI ARTIFACTS

<u>June 16, 1944</u>: Today, I had a chance to examine the Nazi trenches, pillboxes, and machine gun placements. The opening of the pillboxes are a hexagon shape. The walls of the pillbox are at least a foot thick.

A small painting of the area of the view for each gunner is on the wall by the gun emplacement. It has the elevation and range of the beach written in both French and German. Telephone lines and tunnels lead from one pillbox to the next. A number of their larger guns had an absolutely unobstructed view of the beach. Machine guns by the score were dug in deep. They were positioned so that our ships were like sitting ducks on a pond. It is a wonder that we were ever able to take the beach. There is still enough live ammunition, grenades, shells, etc., in the trenches to start another war. When I look at the mountain of empty shell casings, I can't help but think about how many Americans lost their lives because of these guns. Without the splendid shooting of the battleships and destroyers, along with all the soldiers who spent many hours trying to take the beach, this particular beachhead would have been a failure. Eventually, the Germans who manned these guns were wiped out. I feel that the men who have the best chance in this type of warfare are the ship's crews. Unfortunately, it has been confirmed that L.S.T. #314 is indeed gone, with the loss of all hands [*all crew members died*].

I am writing this sitting atop the first hill. I am facing the beach. A makeshift hospital is behind me. The mined gully is to my right. The "city" of a thousand pup tents, that we are calling "strafer's paradise," is to my left. As I look past the waves, I can still see 40 to 50 sunken craft in the surf. I can only see about 250 ships as far as the horizon. That is quite a drop from a few days ago.

CHAPTER
EIGHT

DOING THE JOB

<u>June 16, 1944</u>: Our job with the Rhinos is almost done. Our main purpose of the invasion was to go onto the beach with the First Wave. This craft drafts only inches of water so it could float over the underwater mines that the other boats could not. That and the fact it is made up of many metal pontoons made it virtually unsinkable. However, it is now clear that the amount of guns the Nazis had was vastly underestimated. Thus, it took much longer than expected to silence the guns that were commanding the beach. In addition, rough water and a stern beach master were some of the main obstacles that slowed us up. Thank God. Now I can see how easy it would

have been for the German gunners to just wait and pick their targets at will. We sure were lucky that we didn't advance.

Now that it has been a couple days, and I can gather my thoughts, I will write down more of my experiences with the invasion. I remember starting at the beach at 4:00 AM. Because I was at the helm steering the Tug, I had a very good view of the invasion. With my head held high and my eyes straight ahead, we ran straight for the beach until we almost hit it. Then I began circling one hundred yards off shore, waiting for my next orders. As I waited, I was watching all the action and pointing at targets as they exploded into flame. Shells began landing very near to us, and I began to understand just how dangerous this job was. It is still dangerous now. I did hear that not all of the Rhino crews performed as well under fire.

Four Rhino crew members, including "GOLD BRAIDS" [Naval officers], are up for court martial for deserting their ships and men during the attack. It is 10:00 PM and I just completed my dugout a short while ago, and now I am as snug as a bug. I neglected to mention the living quarters that the Germans had underground. It seems that they lived with their guns for the past 18 months. Apparently, their wives (or mistresses) lived with them.

We found women's slippers in their quarters. It could be that the slippers started that rumor about French women acting as snipers.

CHAPTER
NINE

NAZI COUNTER ATTACK

Headquarters warned us to expect a blitz tonight. We were told the blast of the whistle over the microphone would be the alarm that Nazi paratroopers had landed in our lines.

News says the Nazis are massing by the mouth of the peninsula. It turns out that the Germans did have poison gas, but they never used it on us. The only gas scare proved false.

June 16, 1944: Jerries were over loud and long last night. I don't know if it was 10 separate attacks or one continual raid. Let's just say that stuff really flew. Today I figured out that I have been in the service for one year. From Chicago to France in twelve months of mismanagement. There was no enemy action during the day. We can gamble on them being over tonight again. I have heard that their submarines and mines are doing quite a bit of damage to the "England to France supply route." I heard that another one of our ships had been hit and another thirty Seabees are dead. For me personally, there has been quite a bit of inactivity lately. If this is my job going forward, it is safe to say I have had enough of war. I'm ready to go home. If we are really here to repel paratrooper attacks, why don't we get in a better defensive position? Instead, we are all in one area like a bunch of ants. It is a mystery to me why barracks are located by ammunition dumps. We were directly over one in Plymouth, and we are over one here in France. It will be a sad day if the Jerries locate it and blow up our encampment.

Tomorrow, I have permission to travel inland. We have erected a German prison camp across the road from us. Our camp is practically a prison. We are not allowed anywhere without written orders. The news says that the Nazis have an army of 300,000 men ready to surround our beachhead. If that is the case, we are outnumbered. I also learned that the Germans are using pilotless planes to attack England.

June 17, 1944: I just returned to camp and helped erect a hasty pup tent camp for new troops coming in. A large convoy of troops and supplies is expected soon. I guess we need both badly. A Naval Captain said if there weren't a thousand plane raids on us within 16 days of D-Day (June 22nd), then our invasion would stick.

I heard the British traitor, Haw-Haw, over the airwaves tonight. He said he was broadcasting from the German front. You could hear guns blasting in the background as he reported the butchery of allied troops and the capture of prisoners. It is only pure propaganda.

Not many planes flew over tonight, and I slept through most of the firing. We are all getting awfully filthy. I am so sick of eating out of a can, but I think if I had a fresh vegetable right now, it would make me sick. My body will need a while to get back on track.

The French seem to be taking the invasion "matter of factually." They are not too amiable when they see us. No French flag waving like I thought there would be. It makes me wonder if they really wanted us sticking our noses in their country. I heard the invasion is rumored to have cost us 20,000 men. The graveyard with all of the white little crosses that have been set up on the top of this hill is a pretty sad sight.

This is official: our army is fighting 23 miles into France. The Nazis are trying to stop us from getting our lines across the peninsula, and robot planes are bombing England.

CHAPTER TEN

SCUTTLEBUTT

<u>June 18, 1944</u>: No sight of the big convoy yet. Scuttlebutt has it that we were originally supposed to leave for the United States in September, but now orders are to get the two bags of personal equipment and clothing we left in England sent over here so we can dig in for the winter. Then, just like that, the orders changed again. Now it sounds that the Army Engineers will do the construction work inland. We are supposed to stay on the coast and repair the docks in Cherbourg. If that is the job, we certainly won't be here until next summer.

At 6:30 PM, we just heard word that our troops had cut off the Cherbourg peninsula. This will make it very hard for the Nazis to attack us in force. There was a lot of shooting last night. The First and Second Armies are now in France. The convoy is to bring the badly needed 3rd Army.

It has been 12 days since the invasion. Unfortunately, it was only four days after the invasion when the "Gold Braids" came onshore and started taking over details like wanting the men to line up and muster and other childish tasks.

June 19, 1944: The stuff really dropped last night: rain, mud, bombs, shells. It has been reported that the German pilotless planes are not radio-controlled. After they leave the catapult, the Nazis have no control over them. However, they do carry a 2,000 lb. bomb and can travel at 300 mph, so that can be a little scary. But at least the Germans have not figured out how to guide them to the targets.

Yesterday morning the Lt. Commander said to the chiefs, "No doubt you will hear a lot of scuttlebutt about when we will leave France. You may as well get it straight. We will be here for three to six months. Most likely, it will be six months." At a meeting this afternoon with Navy Captains, Air Corps Majors, and Army Generals, another change was discussed. Unofficially, the pup tent camp is to be a rest camp for the Army when units arrive and leave France. My unit is now scheduled to leave August 1st. A remark was supposed to have been made at the meeting that the 111th Battalion will be the only outfit to be in both theaters of war in one year. I hope this doesn't mean I will be sent to the Pacific rather than the United States when my time here is done.

June 20, 1944: It has been two weeks since the invasion. We shot ten planes down last night. The firing was loud and fast all night. A lot of shrapnel was dropped in our tent city last night. I was supposed to start a

"24-on / 24-off" Rhino unloading duty this morning, but due to extremely rough seas, it was delayed. The raging water has made a wreck of the beach. Millions of dollars worth of government crafts and equipment are being beaten to powder. I was able to walk inland a few miles and talk to a few French who are slowly filtering back to their homes.

June 21, 1944: Another rough day. Waves that are 10 to 15 feet high are sweeping everything sideways on the beach. Only a few enemy planes over last night, none shot down. I'm getting sick and tired of sitting here taking their abuse night after night.

June 22, 1944: It is 12:00 noon. I am on top of a hill watching the sea abate. The sun sticks its rosy head out now and then. It really is a marvelous sight. At 1:00 PM, orders came to dig our foxholes three-and-a-half feet deep for flak protection. I am only able to dig one-and-a-half feet down. The soil is hard and rocky. With the shortage of shovels, it is going to take me a week of digging to get down another two feet. I had my first bath in the past three weeks. It was in a bucket, but it was swell. I threw away all of the clothes I have been wearing since the invasion.

Everyone is so filthy and dirty that I have no doubt I will fit in again in no time. Our drinking water has the rankest taste ever.

I talked to some Rangers, and it seems the war is not as cut and dried as the newscasters would let you believe. Orders just came to prepare ourselves for 24 hours of operation. At 3:00 PM, hundreds of our bombers flew towards Cherbourg to cut the Nazi supply line.

It seems to me that the Nazi plan right now is to use their pilotless bombers to blow out the shipping ports in England. This would cut off supplies and soldiers that reinforce our troops in France. Their E-Boats are already taking a heavy toll on the channel shipping.

If this plan works, our half-a-million troops over here would be doomed. I feel we will overcome whatever losses the Germans give to us by the sheer weight of our numbers. We have more soldiers being brought to the front by the hour. The Liberty Ships and L.S.T.s are unloading without being hampered in the least. The number of lives it will take for victory is secondary. As soon as Cherbourg falls to us, we will most likely abandon this beach for the deepwater port.

June 23, 1944: All bulldozers are to be made shipshape in two days, ready to load aboard an L.S.T. to be taken back to England. The scuttlebutt is that Companies "B" and "C" are going to be called up to make another beachhead. Either on the north coast of France or through Belgium. Some of the boys who had been through D-Day messed their britches when they heard that news.

CHAPTER

ELEVEN

A NEW NORMAL

<u>June 24, 1944</u>: Just returned from our Rhino where I completed over 24 hours of operations. I had a meal aboard a merchant ship. It was the first piece of bread I had eaten in a month. I wish I had joined the Merchant Marines. They take less chances, and make many times the money.

Deckhands make $2,400 on a three-month trip. When I was out, we picked up the body of a sailor. That was one of the most horrible things I have seen since D-Day. He was probably in the water for 15 days and was so waterlogged that he didn't look human.

We did see the Limey beach get bombed unmercifully by the Germans.

June 25, 1944: Enemy bombers were over early and long last night. It looked like the end of the world. Our casualties are all sent to England, and all recovered bodies are buried. There are an awful lot of bodies that have not yet been identified. A storm is expected.

June 26, 1944: Just returned to camp after working on the Rhino. My foxhole/pup tent has inches of water in it. Rain, hard rain, is making life difficult. We are soaked to the skin laying in wet blankets. I have nothing but the cold night and German bombers to look forward to tonight.

June 27, 1944: Misery. A night that was soaked through and through. It rained so hard that even Jerry decided not to show up (I guess that was a good thing). It stopped raining about noon, so we laid our blankets out to dry, and it began to rain again. Another time, it stopped, so we took our gear out of the tent, and then it really poured. It rained so hard that the tent fell down on me. I put the tent back up, and it is still raining. Woe is me!

June 28, 1944: Bombers were over again last night. The shelling kept me awake. I found out some interesting news from "The Man" in the briefing. It seems that company "E" was in the 111th Battalion a few weeks before D-Day. It was to be used to replace our "B" Company. The reason was the military's "bean counters" estimated that 60% or more of our Rhino crews were expected to be lost in the invasion. Imagine their shock when we only suffered a fraction of the expected losses. Now, they have a whole company of men sitting back in England, waiting for us to die.

The only resistance left on this strip of land is off to the right. I am sure that as soon as Cherbourg Harbor is secure, we will move our focus there. I hope so. As if things couldn't get worse. Yesterday, while it was still raining, the officers walked around "tent city" and took our shelter halves that we had been using for flooring. Now, the dirt is caked on us in layers. The mud just rolls right on us as we attempt to sleep. The chaplain even complained to Commander Jardin, but to no avail. Even though mud had overtaken the tent he was using it for church services.

Official reports of the landing were disclosed. Of the casualties and deaths; Americans 24,000, English 13,000 and Canadian 2,000 [*These were the facts as Bob knew them at the time and may not be accurate*]. This burns me up! The stinking British have the nerve to broadcast to the world that they contributed three ships to every one of ours during the invasion. Before D-Day, they said that 90% of the assault force losses would be from the English. The Canadians would lose 60% during the invasion, and the Americans were expected to lose 10% of their men. That was before the shuffle where the Americans got the three-mile beach with four layers of mine-laden obstacles. By any standard, we had the toughest beach by far. But since we did not have complete control of the beach in under 36 hours, the English were asking, "What is the trouble?" Two days later, we had to travel to their beach to get them out of a murderous German trap where they had surrounded the beach. The British often seem to hate and belittle Americans, and I must say that it is becoming mutual.

CHAPTER
TWELVE

SEABEES

I want to recognize the men on the Rhino and the Tug who were crew with me on D-Day. Tug: Behee, Camere, Yacovone, Fisher, Sullivan, Zelmanski, Fabela, and Robertson. RHINO: Schutt, Hardy, Post, Hill, Reeves, Schonwetter, Rothemel, Sifritt, Duval, Prowell, Hull, Hakman, Forsythe, Bloodworth, Farwell, Mattke, Denham.

June 29, 1944: I just completed over twenty-four hours duty on the new Rhino #32. We unloaded the British ship "Wildrose". I had a long talk with a British lad. I understand a lot more now. Of the 1,500 Seabees in the 111th Battalion, only 230 actually participated on the day of the invasion. Yet there is talk of a citation for the entire battalion. So even though only a few took the risks and spilled their blood, all will be rewarded.

At 8:00 PM, one can almost set their watch on the nightly arrival of the German planes. I am lying on the cold pontoons watching the bombers and the shells hit the beach. The attitude of the guys right now, with a few exceptions, is if we are going to get killed, we are going to get killed. It is not worth hiding every time you hear an explosion. Even if it happens to be hitting close by. This does not mean we want to take unnecessary risks, just that we are accepting fate.

Food here is very bad. However, through the quick fingers of some members of our crew, you can usually find fresh fruit and juices hidden in our tents. There is a loud-speaker system set up in camp. In the evening the radio is playing over it. We hear rebroadcasts of American news, both on the

BBC and NBC. According to the news, we have the enemy on the run in Europe. The more I think of it, the more I think news of us being sent to the South Pacific eventually is more than a rumor. As I write this, I hear the growl of our big guns (at least, I hope they are ours).

CHAPTER

THIRTEEN

A HARD RAIN

June 30, 1944: Big storm hitting. Within 10 minutes, my foxhole had inches of water in it. During a let-up, I moved the tent to higher ground. Let the shrapnel fly. I am not going to dig another hole to get flooded every few days. Six German robot plane catapults have been captured. It's a damn good thing we invaded before the Nazis had a chance to turn them loose on England. I am quite sure they would have blown the mountain of supplies that we were loading to smithereens. Not to mention, the psychological effect of pilotless bombs falling on us all hours of the day and night would have been terrible. There are hundreds of B-17 Flying Fortresses flying over me as I write this. They have been flying over me in formation for over 30 minutes. This must be a record raid. The enemy must be trembling with such mighty firepower coming at them. I am glad they are ours.

What an awesome sight! It is strange for me to watch the planes fly over, then sometime later, watch them fly back. Then we turn on the radio and wait for the broadcast of what they did and where they hit. As I write this, I can still see the last plane heading to Germany. At the same time, in the far distance I can see the first planes returning. I plan to hear plenty about this raid real soon. I hope that they caught Hitler's troops before they were able to hit us in full force. Apparently, the overconfident Germans told the French that they would be back manning the guns on the beach in 10 days after we drove them out. Well, it has been almost a month, and I don't see any Germans except the ones in the prison camp. I did see an elderly French woman clomping around in an old pair of huge G.I. boots. I feel that the French resent us. They definitely hate the English, and the English hate them. War is so useless and terrible. According to the news, we are supposed to control the peninsula, yet just now, I watched German big guns, not more than five miles away, fire at our planes flying back.

July 1, 1944: I am aboard the Rhino, trying to get loads of trucks to the shore in the rain (of course). That rumor about Jap [*slang term for Japanese soldier*] prisoners being imported to teach the Nazis better sniping techniques appears to be true. Snipers seem to be behind each hedge and tree. It is proving costly in both lives and time for the Americans to take out the snipers. When we read in the papers that German and Italian prisoners back home are getting schooling, candy, and even a quart of beer a day, it makes our blood boil. You can bet your life that our boys, who are their prisoners, are getting nothing but abuse. The big convoy finally arrived last night with lots of reinforcements. Of course, Jerry flew over to welcome them.

July 2, 1944: I am back at camp again. There are bright flashes in the sky and there has been heavy fighting in the direction of Cherbourg. The Germans really seem to be fighting in force off to my left. The news says nothing about the battle. This probably means we are deadlocked or being pushed back. This war feels like a long way from being won.

However, I have seen several thousand troops being landed in the past week, so we are definitely taking the fight to the Germans.

July 4, 1944: I am back at camp. I just completed 24 hours of sleepless operations. There was a full moon last night that made us an inviting target to Jerry to the tune of five raids. The last one ended about 5:15 AM. In addition to the planes, an artillery duel lit the sky all night. And, of course, it's raining again.

<u>July 5, 1944</u>: It is still raining, and I am heading back to the Rhino for 48 hours of operations.

CHAPTER
FOURTEEN

D-DAY + ONE MONTH

<u>July 6, 1944</u>: It has been one month since D-Day. I can't remember if I explained why the 111th Battalion decided to form an "E" company or not. Here is the latest insult. Company "E" was formed without much fanfare to replace our Company "B" Rhino operators. The leaders figured we would be butchered on D-Day. But it looks like the commanders "counted their chickens before they were hatched." Now, even though Company "E" did not see any action on D-Day (because "B" Company was not destroyed), they are scheduled to get a citation for bravery.

The situation for us may be getting worse. The men on the Liberty Ships we unload are telling me that they keep seeing shipload after shipload of metal pontoons being delivered to England. The scuttlebutt is they are being used to put together more Tugs and Rhinos for another invasion. It is my fear that they would like to put those with the experience of landing during D-Day in charge of this new invasion.

In all of the magazines I have seen, they mention D-Day and the beach landings in lengthy detail (without somehow mentioning the bodies that I saw stacked three deep on the beach). However, I have seen no mention anywhere of the contributions of the Seabees to the invasion and getting men and supplies on the beach. Someone from the battalion should contact a reporter and tell him what we have done here for the past month. Our overall casualty list is going up because of deaths due to flak wounds.

<u>July 7, 1944</u>: I am still on the Rhino. We saw five "flying bombs" last night in the space of a half hour. At a great height, they appear as a star. At lower levels, they look like a plane that is on fire. We did see one get shot down. It kept getting brighter and brighter, like it was heading for us. Reports say that over 2,500 have been launched in England in two weeks. That comes to over five million pounds of TNT. It is a lucky thing we got most of our equipment out of England and over here in France when we did. After we take over more of France, we will offer a larger target, and the Germans will use the flying bombs against us. They can kill more men accidentally than most bombs do on purpose. I am back in my pup tent at 7:00 PM. We have heard that the Germans are using oil-filled rocket shells to start fires in the ranks.

<u>July 8, 1944</u>: Jerry swooped low over our tents time and time again. Luckily, we were able to shoot a plane down before it

could drop its bombs on us. We hear the news broadcasts, and I have figured that when reporters don't say much about Normandy, and I can hear a huge battle being waged a few miles from me, it means we are getting pushed back and losing ground. If that is the case, things must not be going so good right now for the allies.

<u>July 9, 1944</u>: I am leaving in a few minutes for the 48 hours of operation on the Rhino. A Nazi soldier was captured in a hidden pillbox. He had been hiding there for over a month. I am not sure what he was eating, but he looked pretty skinny.

It is remarkable to me how unfair the distribution of medals is. It seems that only officers get them. Enlisted men only get them posthumously or when they are M.I.A., which is usually the same thing when you are talking sea duty. The men who do the actual deeds are looked at as a gun to be ordered by a commander, miles from the actual objective. I believe numerous acts of heroism must be performed to accomplish even the smallest mission. Then, when the mission is a success, the officer takes all the credit.

CHAPTER
FIFTEEN

HEARING GABRIEL'S HORN

ACHTUNG MINEN! [*German for "Attention Mines"*]. At 6:00 PM today, "I heard Gabriel's horn." After they found that German in the pillbox, my friend Zel and I decided to see if we could find any more hidden pillboxes within the cliffs. After a lengthy search, the only thing of note that we found was a rotten Nazi arm on the ground.

We had a little trouble tracing our way down the cliff. As I stepped onto a path, there was a terrific explosion. One that was strong enough to knock us both to the ground. I knew we had set off a mine. I felt a burning sensation in my right leg. I kept my eyes closed because I was sure that if I looked, I would see my leg was blown off. I have seen the effects that mines have on people, and most of the time, they are torn apart. As I opened my eyes, I was able to see that, miraculously, I seemed to be in one piece. As I picked myself up, I saw Zel next to me with blood streaming down his face. He was crawling and trying to get to his feet. Both of us looked at each other with a dazed look. I asked him if he was hurt. He replied that he had got it in his legs.

Before I could respond to Zel, the ground began to tremble. A noise, too loud for me to perceive, thundered in my ears. Then I was shot up into the air and was flung by the concussion of the blast into a trench some ten feet away. When I opened my eyes this time, I saw that Zel had been thrown into the trench with me. Both of us were bruised and battered but very much alive! My leg was numb at this point, and I tried to ignore it because I was sure that it must be in critical shape. We sat there talking it over before either of us tried to move and examine how bad we were hurt.

Zel was blotting the blood off of his face. With the blood he felt going down his chin, it took me a while to reassure him that he only had a tiny wound. Both of us were practically deaf, with a loud ringing in our left ears from the tremendous explosion.

Demolition officers who were inspecting the area came over to us and expressed great surprise to find anyone alive. Their surprise was only surpassed by the army doctors when they saw two men walk into a hospital who had not just stepped on a mine, but the explosion from the mine had set off an unexploded bomb that was in the ground. We were the talk of the base for a while. Soldiers would look at us walk by like they were witnessing an actual miracle. The scientists did not credit our escape to God but to the fact that we were too close to the second explosion and rather than becoming incinerated in the bomb's explosion, the concussive waves pushed us away from the rest of the explosion.

Both of us have headaches, scratches, and punctures on our bodies from head to toe. Both of us also have some large bruises on our legs and back. Zel's left eye is sore, but he can see. My left ear is very painful, and I am not sure if I will be able to hear out of it again. My body is very sore overall.

The demolition officers told us that if the bomb's blast concussion had tossed us in the opposite direction a few feet, we would have been thrown off the hundred-foot cliff to our deaths. I have seen both Army and Navy doctors. At the hospital, our eyes were bathed, our wounds probed for shrapnel, and we were given a tetanus shot for lockjaw.

Then they made me and Zel walk miles back to our foxholes for the night. We are to see the doctors again tomorrow for a check-up.

I feel kind of silly relating this incident to anyone because it is so unbelievable. All of us have seen men torn limb from limb with tiny S-Mines. People told us that they heard the bomb's explosion miles around. Maybe it was a true miracle. I guess I should go to church more.

CHAPTER
SIXTEEN

WOUNDED BACK ON DUTY

July 10, 1944: I saw the doctor at 9:30 AM. He told me I had a perforated eardrum, but I would be able to work with it. He did not give me any time off. At 1:00 PM, I was back on the Rhino. My ear is really bothering me, and I try not to get it wet. Any noise seems to get to me. I think my nerves might still be affected by the experience.

July 11, 1944: I am back in tent city. I really have a case of the nerves since the accident. During the nightly raid last night, my nerves were C-string tight at each explosion. Ordinarily, I relax and usually sleep as I am resigned to my fate. My feeling is if the bombs and shells are directed at me, there is nothing I can do about it. There still isn't anything I can do about them, but now, at each burst, I tense up and relive that horrible explosion. Perhaps I will get used to it in time. I am currently deaf in my left ear. I saw the newsreels of the landing that they are showing to the people back home. It must have been very difficult for them to have edited all of the wreckage and dead bodies from the film. It is almost funny.

July 16, 1944: It is raining again. There was an awfully big raid last night. The battle sounds like it is close. I heard that three men were killed by mines.

July 17, 1944: Leaving for 48 hours to work on the Rhino. Nothing seems important enough for me to write about any longer. Air raids, ships shelling, bombs, mines, flying bombs; they have all become matters of fact at this point. Mail from home is all that is important to me now.

July 19, 1944: At camp again. A huge battle is being waged within earshot. The Germans are waging a counterattack around Caen. I counted 13 air raids the other foggy night. I watched the German planes dropping mines into the harbor. All of the ships have been ordered not to fire on the planes unless they are hit to save ammunition. The shore batteries have been pretty effective in knocking down some planes. My nerves have quieted some. I am still deaf in my left ear, but I have begun to hear some ringing, so I hope my hearing will begin to return soon.

July 23, 1944: I just returned from duty. A storm kept us company most of the time. It was not as severe as the "tornado" that knocked the tent camp down a few weeks ago. However, my tent was knocked down again, and everything was soaked. The rain battered us pretty badly. During the storm, we were reminded of what happened on June 6th when bodies and body parts began washing ashore from D-Day. A Rhino tied up next to ours had the upper half of a man wash aboard. We were instructed to remove the identification and throw the remains overboard. His head was as big as a basketball.

I was on watch last night. The clouds were very low, so that meant that the Jerries came in very low. I was really afraid of getting bombed, but it seemed like the planes were only dropping mines. At times, the firing of our guns was tremendous. A fire bright enough to light up the entire horizon was blazing and exploding for hours.

CHAPTER
SEVENTEEN

MOVING TO
UTAH BEACH

We have been told to move five Rhinos from Omaha Beach to Utah Beach. This is the first time that I will be going to a different beach since D-Day. While the Rhino and Tug motored to Utah Beach, me and the rest of the crew came to Utah Beach overland by truck.

Our trip was 50 miles in length, through many towns. Isigny was the largest city. Our bombs have caused massive devastation in these towns, as the Nazis have in England. Very few shops are open, but the people seem friendly to us. Young children unknowingly give us the Nazi salute like they were taught to by the Germans. I saw a burned glider by the road, along with the wreckage of other planes in a field. An area that looked about two miles long was pockmarked with craters of gigantic proportions. There was a steady stream of French vehicles on the road trying to get to safety, wherever that was.

July 25, 1944: I am aboard a Rhino on Utah Beach. There were two L.S.T. and one Liberty Ship sunk here. It is obvious to me why our beach (Omaha) was the toughest. This beach is as flat as a plate. There are very few places the Germans could put gun emplacements. The Jerries bombed here last night. Along with the bombs, they dropped tinsel strips in the air to foul our Radar. We are expecting a large raid tonight. I went to visit some of the surrounding villages: Carentan, Volongnes, and Montebourg. I am sure they were lovely before the war, but they are all in shambles now. I did not see one building in Montebourg that was untouched by the war. As we drove closer to Cherbourg,

I could see that the tremendous fortress atop the mountain seemed to be hardly touched by war. The city of Cherbourg also seemed intact. I bought a deck of cards and some other souvenirs there. I think the Americans have taken over Cherbourg with our Francs. The port also looks good. I have heard this is the best farmland in all of France. It certainly looks prosperous to me. The countryside is beautiful. All of the fields seem to be yielding healthy crops, with horses, chickens, and cattle galore. This is more amazing when one understands this is in the middle of a brutal war. I see that in most of the fields, the Germans had pounded in posts at intermittent levels to hamper the landings of our gliders, planes, and paratroopers. The Germans were smart, and there is a glider in a field that looks to have hit some of these obstacles and crashed.

July 27, 1944: I am back onboard the Rhino, awaiting relief. Apparently, it rains on this beach too, because it is really coming down now. Allied ships have been purposely scuttled here to form a breakwater. The planes are still coming over every night, dropping bombs and mines.

On my tour the other day, I forgot to report that I saw the wreckage of a German Mark IV Panzer *[Tank]*. I also saw the remains of some two-man tanks and cars. Their automobiles seem to be a little smaller than the Austins in England.

The two bags I left in England before D-Day arrived today. Unfortunately, they were sent to Omaha Beach (where I am not).

It does not feel that I will be getting home to the States for a long time, but we did just get some good news. On July 25th, the Allies finally broke through the German lines and cemented our invasion. That was the good news I have been waiting to hear for a long time. Now, I am finally beginning to feel secure.

CHAPTER
EIGHTEEN

FRED

No sooner had I put my pencil down an explosion shook the air around me at around 8:30 PM. The concussion was so strong that it nearly knocked the pup tent down around me. I heard shouts for help a few seconds after the blast. I slipped on my shoes and went running on the road toward the cries. An M.P. shouted at me and told me to stop moving because the field was mined. I got so shaky that I was not sure I was going to be able to retrace my steps. As I got back to the road, I noticed two men carrying a bloody pulp. They asked me to help them get an ambulance. I was able to stop a Jeep, and I commandeered it to the proper place. The two men brought the man out, laying him across the hood of the Jeep. He was in rough shape. His left arm was blown off at the elbow, one side of his face (including his teeth) were blown away, and his legs were just two bloody stumps.

Practically all of his clothing was torn off him. When I took another look at him, I saw that it was a man from Company "B" named Fred. It looked like the same type of mine that Zel and I had stepped on had got him.

July 28, 1944: Fred died last night. He left a wife and three children behind. Nobody is really sure what the hell he was doing out in that field. However, due to the fact that he was out of bounds without permission, his insurance will not cover his death.

The 81st Battalion, whom we are helping here on Utah Beach, got an eight-day leave to go back to England starting today. We got nothing.

CHAPTER
NINETEEN

WAR IS NOT FAIR

My nerves must be calming down, or maybe I just don't care anymore. There was a bad raid here last night. I heard the shots and explosions, but I slept through most of it. I found out in the morning that the anti-aircraft guns next to my camp were silent because Jerry knocked out the Radar. Then they strafed the road near us, killing three men and knocking out a truck. Tonight, I will try to pay more attention.

July 30, 1944: On the Rhino, waiting to go back to the beach, but the tide is not right, so I must wait longer. The biggest air raid since we arrived took place yesterday.

The entire sky was filled with tracers and bursts. Quite a number of the German planes were shot down. It lasted for hours, and the ground shook with the shock from our exploding guns. Nothing was bombed near us. Although, I did have quite a scare. I heard a loud whizzing and fluttering sound coming in the direction of my tent. I slumped as low as I could, expecting an explosion. But I only heard the loud "thud" of a piece of flak hitting the ground. It must have been a very big piece to make such a loud noise. During a raid, I still get an occasional sense of fright, thinking that tonight is when my luck will be used up. I just think with all of the raids that I have sat through the law of averages will catch up to me sometime. Well, let's hope not. Maybe I will be relieved soon.

July 31, 1944: I am really mad. Yesterday, when we gave our lines to a Liberty ship as we were docking to them, the merchant seaman did not receive them. He let G.I. soldiers grab them instead. It seems that since it was Sunday, the civilian seaman was able to refuse to work unless he was paid double-time pay. Time and again, I've noticed that when we tie up to a ship after 5:00 PM, an officer of the ship or Army soldier will take and secure the lines. This is true even if the ship's civilian crew is hanging over the side of the ship and has to duck to avoid our lines. They will not touch a line for less than time and a half pay after 5:00 PM. THIS IS ON A BATTLEFRONT IN THE MIDDLE OF A WAR!! When they touch a line (before 5:00 and not on a Sunday), they will do absolutely nothing but secure their ship. That consists of dropping an anchor. During an air raid the other night, the Armed Guard from the Navy asked two men from the Liberty ship's crew to help man the guns. They refused, and the captain of their ship backed them up. THIS WAS WHEN THE ENEMY WAS OVERHEAD, DROPPING MINES AND BOMBS ON THEM! They also refuse to give us a cup of coffee after evening chow because the one who poured it would demand and receive overtime pay. Now that it's so vividly brought to my attention, I recall all the insults the Liberty ship's crews make to members serving in the armed forces; I ask myself, "Why doesn't the Navy just man the ships?" It would be heaven. I would have warm, comfortable quarters, showers, sanitation, fresh vegetables, and meat. I would gladly take a cut in pay from my $15 a month for the privilege to work on one of those ships. I have heard that the lowliest toilet cleaner or bed orderly on a Liberty ship makes $350 a month, not counting overtime pay. In addition, they get a bonus for each day they are in a foreign port. They also get an additional bonus for just sitting through an attack.

The Company commander told us today, "I'll have some important news for you men soon." I hope he will be telling us that we will be getting eight days' leave like the 81st Battalion. I'm not going to hold my breath.

He did tell us that he fought the higher-ups so that Fred's widow will be able to get his $10,000 life insurance. So that is a good thing.

<u>August 2, 1944</u>: We are beached aboard the Rhino. A storm has started, and we will be on the beach until it subsides. "Fighting French" troops from England landed last night. We also saw several truckloads of Nazi prisoners being taken off the beach.

I have a gripe. It seems that our great democracy is not the least bit democratic where our service is concerned. The other day, cots were sent to our camp for the Chiefs [*Chief Petty officers are a senior enlisted rank in the Navy*] to sleep on. Large tents, with enough room to house eight men, are being used by two Chiefs to sleep on. While we sleep "in" the ground. At the 111th camp, the men dug trenches and holes for the officer's tents. Tents were erected and floors put in for the Chiefs and officers alike. I was ordered to stop setting up my pup tent and to dig in for the "Gold Braid." I refused because it would be impossible to finish my job in the dark. An air raid at the time clinched my argument. Chiefs are given private tents to eat in, while officers have a private chow hall with better food. The enlisted men have to eat on the ground in all sorts of weather.

At the 111th camp, I ate from the chow hall three times out of a possible 126 times. That's how deplorable the conditions were. During the heat of battle, the officers would detail a man to bring food to them so that they did not have to take a risk. There have been court martials when enlisted men spoke up. I speak up too often. I don't think I will get a court martial, but I am disliked by the higher-ups.

<u>August 5, 1944</u>: Some nasty-looking fleshy debris that was once a man washed ashore today. On another matter, I have left my upper and lower lip unshaven since D-Day. I am sporting a pretty good beard. I doubt I will be able to smuggle it home, but I

would like to, just for the laughs I would get when people back home laid eyes on me since I left for war. There has been no mail for some time.

August 7, 1944: It is 11:30 PM, and there is a fair amount of bombing going on now. It still gives me a little fear that the planes flying at night are Nazi planes. Since it is hard to see them at night, they always sound much lower than they actually are. One plane is circling overhead now. I'm on watch, but I am not sure what I am really watching out for.

CHAPTER
TWENTY

LEAVING FRANCE

<u>August 12, 1944</u>: Hundreds of tanks landed on the beach yesterday. It looks like they will soon have a surprise for the Nazis. Eight of our Rhinos are being sent to Cherbourg. Unfortunately, Zel keeps hurting himself. He received first and second-degree burns while working on the Rhino. He spent the entire day in the hospital, but he should be alright. Many people have been saying that they are going to close down this beach and send us elsewhere. There were several bombs dropped the last few nights, but I don't see any damage that they caused.

<u>August 15, 1944</u>: We found a Rhino yesterday afternoon that was high and dry on the beach. The tide came in right about the time a big storm hit with high winds.

We battled for hours to keep the Rhino from being broached. I was wet to the bone as the waves washed high over us. The tide is now out, but I know we will have this same struggle in a couple of hours if we can't get this Rhino off the beach. My ear has been troublesome for me. I plan to have somebody look at it if there is an opportunity. The latest scuttlebutt is that we will go back to the United States for leave, but then we leave for a new assignment in the South Pacific.

<u>August 24, 1944</u>: The Jerries came a little early today at 5:00 PM. They paid for this by getting two of their planes shot down. We are leaving our Rhino here at Utah Beach and heading back to Omaha Beach tomorrow.

<u>September 14, 1944</u>: Usual stuff, I broke my finger and the Germans keep attacking us every night. There are literally hundreds

of German prisoners that are being sent to England. I finally saw the doctor about my ear and he told me it is torn too bad to heal. When I complained about the pain I get when I hear loud noises, he said harshly, "Plug up your ear so you don't hear the loud noises." So much for the doctor fixing me.

September 18, 1944: Here are some things I hate about officers: well-heated accommodations, furniture, radio, individual showers, elite chow hall, bar and officers club, private parties, weekly dances with nurses and WACS. This is all very detrimental to the enlisted men's morale. This is causing a lot of insubordination, which you can't have in a war. The officers have only offered us a few days of liberty in Paris to offset the men's resentment of their parties. The officers have had official liberty since Cherbourg was taken several months ago.

A man was busted up in an auto-wreck. He is now laying in the hospital. No attempt has been made to X-ray him with his busted arm. The doctor said, "If we get to Cherbourg, I'll have him X-rayed." He's been suffering for two weeks now without proper treatment.

By October 1944, most of the 111th Battalion had been shipped back to the United States. But "B" Company, who had been manning the Rhinos in France, were sent back to England. Leave was proposed for travel within England, and I had made arrangements to visit my relatives, the Millers, in Scotland. That was until the Battle of the Bulge. All leave was canceled. I was immediately shipped back to the United States on a stormy sea. My ear had "miraculously" healed. So, any chance of a medical discharge was gone. I was given a 30-day leave and then shipped to the South Pacific to carry on the war, still with the 111th Battalion Seabees.

CHAPTER
TWENTY-ONE

SHIPPING OUT AGAIN

Editor's Note: Robert G. Behee continued the diary he began in March 1944. Like his European diary, we have included slang and racist terminology that was common speech back in the 1940s. As editors, we provide links and commentary when what Bob was saying needs to be clarified. As you might imagine, Bob was furious about being thrust into another theater of war after he was almost killed in Europe.

<u>January 1, 1945</u>: I'm on my way back to war after a 30-day leave in the United States.

<u>January 11, 1945</u>: I have never been so downhearted in my life. I am just a cog in the Navy machine. I have just been sitting here disgusted. I was not even able to really enjoy Christmas back home like I thought I would. We are sailing soon.

<u>January 15, 1945</u>: We left Dansville at 2:30 AM by rail. I boarded the U.S.S. Chase in Boston. We are planning to be underway this evening.

<u>January 18, 1945</u>: As we docked in Norfolk, Virginia, I watched a man on the dock get crushed under a huge beam as they were attempting to load a ship. This is not a good omen. I slept in the open hatch all night in the freezing cold. The ship's crew dropped the anchor, chain and all, to the bottom. What a "green" [*inexperienced*] crew! Due to all the time and experience I got from my time in Europe, I am now a M.A.A.[*Master-at-Arms*]. It is good to be a boss. This advancement not

only increased my pay, but also my status. I can now eat early chow. Otherwise, I would have to stand in line for an hour. Our new Ensign Officers are really "boots" [*someone right out of boot camp*]. They range in age from 19-24 years old. They have absolutely no idea of the rugged life and action that is in front of them. One has not even started shaving yet. Wow! We are set to sail at 7:00 PM.

January 19, 1945: A large aircraft carrier and several other ships that are as yet unidentified are with us as we plow towards Panama.

January 21, 1945: We must be by Florida. It's such beautiful, warm, calm weather that I'm actually enjoying the trip so far. I had a terrible dream last night. I am lucky I did not wake up screaming. I dreamt that my right arm was being amputated at the elbow, and I was watching it happen.

CHAPTER
TWENTY-TWO

ENTERING THE PACIFIC THEATER

<u>January 23, 1944</u>: We are in Panama. A few days ago, the sea breeze was perfect, but now it is stiflingly hot. It is almost unbearable to be below deck. We are allowed to sleep on the open deck at night, but the tropical rains usually drive us inside. When we got to the canal, we were marched ashore in platoons.

Panama is a beautiful country. I think that I would like to take a trip here after the war to spend some more time. I had Coca-Cola and ice cream (made in Chicago). There is no tobacco shortage here. It seems that everyone is smoking. We were off the ship for only

30 minutes. We were able to get through the locks by 12:15 AM.

February 1, 1945: We are still rolling to Pearl Harbor, but we seem to have lost the rest of the convoy. We are set to dock in Hawaii next Wednesday. I have to tell you that the sunrises and sunsets in this part of the world are indescribably beautiful. I just had a shot and a vaccination to prepare my body for God knows what.

February 5, 1945: The food is beginning to become inedible. We are still sailing alone, not even a destroyer to keep us company. Scuttlebutt says that our mission has been changed, as the war seems to be advancing so fast. We were originally slated for the Manila detail. Our Company is definitely an invasion unit. The crews are already picked. However, I have no idea what crew I am on.

February 7, 1945: We arrived in Pearl Harbor, Hawaii, last night. I can still see some of the damage from the attack that got us into this mess which has not gotten cleaned up. There is a tremendous fleet here. We were given liberty in Honolulu. I went to Aunt May's house in Waikiki. This really is a beautiful country.

February 11, 1945: We are taking on a few hundred more amphibious troops. This is really crowding the ship. There seems to be hardly enough room to turn around. While things were uncomfortable before, they are downright unbearable now. We are drinking 10% salt water to conserve our fresh water.

February 19, 1945: I have been aboard this ship for five weeks, and I am so fed up with everything that I could just gag.

It's hotter than blazes. I can't get over how inhumane the living conditions are for us. Chow is bad. Water is only turned on at five 15-minute increments for the entire day (for enlisted personnel). Everyone is smelly, dirty, and angry. A body, either Japanese native or American Negro, floated by our ship as we pulled out of Pearl a few days ago. We are no longer traveling alone. An aircraft carrier pulled up to us after exchanging signals. We put a small boat over the side and sent two of our doctors to the aircraft carrier. It appears she had picked up some survivors from a ship that had been sunk and needed some extra doctors. I have been told that we should be able to see land soon. The sea is calm right now.

February 20, 1945: We arrived at the Marshall Islands for a stop. Until recently, these islands were controlled by the Japanese. Now, we have complete control of the islands. There are so many American ships anchored all around the islands. In addition, it seems that our planes are patrolling around the islands 24 hours a day.

CHAPTER
TWENTY-THREE

LIVING IN
THE PHILIPPINES

<u>February 23, 1945</u>: We are underway again to go to war. Half of the convoy left us. I think they may be headed to Guam. I heard that we were originally supposed to go with them, but due to some changes with the war, we will be heading to the Philippines.

<u>March 4, 1945</u>: We sighted some of the Philippine Islands last night. We cruised around, by, and through the islands all day. At 6:15 PM, we moored in Leyte Gulf. We all thought we would be heading to Samar, but it looks like we will be in Leyte for a little while. We had air raids all night. I think

we lost at least one ship. The Japs are still holed up in some of the mountains in the Philippines.

March 8, 1945: We moved to a small island 30 miles outside of Leyte called Calicoan. Most of the 111th Battalion went ashore last night. My duties kept me aboard the ship. From what I hear, the island is deplorable.

March 9, 1945: The men arrived at the campsite without a bag or gear in the wee hours of the morning. As the ship was unloaded, all of the gear was dumped in the center of a clearing. Men slept on the ground around all of this stuff in the pouring rain, followed by the torrid sun. Philippine natives would stroll around us saying, "Hello Joe," and grinning, showing their mouths full of teeth. As we began to erect our cots and tents, the natives would be around asking us for food or cigarettes. They began to teach us important native words like "Pom Pom" [*prostitute*] and "Saki" [*type of alcohol*].

The officer's beauty rest mattresses, flooring, and numerous other extras were soon present to the enlisted men's ire. K-Rations and C-Rations, along with lengthy lines and a chaotic serving system, made meal time an undernourished ordeal. I have been told the present location of our tents is temporary. There is to be more substantial housing constructed for us soon. I will believe it when I see it. The commander said, "We will be here for only two months. As soon as we make our camp livable, we will rest up before the new big invasion." I think that it will take the better part of two months to complete the camp. We are facing an acute water shortage. So, how did the Navy respond? By issuing tropical sun helmets and sunglasses to all hands. Sure, we are thirsty, but we don't have the sun in our eyes. Shirts have been shed, and pants legs shortened. A short time after stepping foot on the island, everyone resembled the movie version of "Jungle Jim." The weather pattern on the island is rain, more rain, then blazing sun, then more rain.

The natives are a constant presence and can be annoying. "Hello, Joe. Do you need help with your laundry?"

<u>March 10, 1945</u>: Island living has not been good for me. There are scorpions and huge centipedes galore. I think one must have got me because my knee is swollen to twice its normal size and is quite painful. The doctor won't even look at it. He says it should go away on its own in a few days. There have been heavy showers all day. Someone told me that the rainy season does not officially start until April. I think I might start to grow gills by May.

<u>March 12, 1945</u>: We stood in a chow line in the driving rain. When we got our chow, we had to eat in the open with our mess kits on the ground. The rain splashed on our food and garbage. All the while, a short distance from us, officers ate under a dry mess tent. Laughing at us eating our soaked food. One young 19-year-old Ensign laughed and

pointed at me as he ate his food on a plate under a canvas, while being waited on.

<u>March 13, 1945</u>: We tried to watch a movie outside. It rained every few minutes. The picture was in eight reels that took five minutes to change, but we stayed to watch the entire movie. We were completely soaked by the end, but it was nice to have a little piece of American culture to take away the loneliness.

We are definitely "not in Kansas anymore." There are young native girls who appear to be only 14 or 15 and are definitely pregnant. Young boys literally run around naked. The girls wear dresses that look like they were made from mattress covers. I heard a rumor that a man brought his wife and daughter to the camp and offered to sell them both for thirty pesos (about fifteen dollars) for one night. Anyway, there were no takers.

There are 800 of us on a 24-hour alert. In other words, we will only get a 24-hour warning before we have to report to the front.

We have to be ready to go at all times. The Japanese still have 14 air bases within 6 to 20 minutes of us. I expect an attack from them once we build up more supplies and they know where we are.

March 18, 1945: A year ago today, I was in South Wales, England, getting prepared for the D-Day invasion. Although there was really no way one could ever get emotionally prepared for the invasion. You just relied on your common sense and luck, trying not to get killed. That is what a lot of these young "Boots" are going to find out really soon if we invade Japan.

March 20, 1945: Many men are in our temporary hospital with yellow fever, malaria, and dysentery. There is barely enough room to accommodate them all.

This is calling all of us to speed up work on building a more permanent hospital. You can add boa constrictors and coral snakes to the list of things that make island living fun.

March 24, 1945: Things are beginning to happen. Thirty men left via air two days ago. They were fully armed for combat. We have been told that 140 men from "B" Company will leave today or tomorrow. We are being assigned to the 5th Fleet Task Force. We know that there will be two more invasions scheduled in the near future. Our "be ready date" is March 29th.

CHAPTER
TWENTY-FOUR

LEAVING TO FIGHT THE JAPANESE

<u>April 1, 1945</u>: We are still here. "Tokyo Rose" may have helped us inadvertently. On her broadcast today, she said, "The boys on Calicoan Island were going to get an Easter present." So we went on high alert, thinking we would get a huge air attack today. Everyone had their carbines, and extra ammo was issued to all hands. Later in the night, 500 Japanese troops landed on Calicoan and began roaming around the island.

<u>April 5, 1945</u>: Well, the Japs tried to take our island, but we were ready for them. After some limited fighting, the Japs were pushed

back, and they sailed away. We are worried they might regroup with larger numbers and try to come back and attack. I still can't get over that "Tokyo Rose" forewarned us, or there would have been many more casualties.

April 12, 1945: Finally got the call to arms. We were given two hours to pack and leave the island. I boarded an L.C.I. with only my battle gear and pack. We arrived at Tacloban and boarded an L.S.T. #941 with 20 men. I believe that we are headed to the "Admiralties."

April 14, 1945: We are en route as part of a huge convoy heading South. Every type of ship conceivable is with us. We are to stop and pick up pontoons to help construct a causeway in Mankin Island. We have so many men and supplies in the L.S.T. The pontoons are going to have to be attached to the outside. When we get to the beach, we will have to secure the pontoons and create a causeway so that the L.S.T. will be able to unload the rest of its load. Scuttlebutt is that we will be using this as a jumping off point to invade Borneo.

<u>April 19, 1945</u>: We crossed the equator, and I was initiated into King Neptune's Royal Order of the Shellbacks. I don't want to talk about what was done. Suffice it to say that it is a rough procedure I will never forget.

<u>April 26, 1945</u>: Arrived in Los Negros. I left L.S.T. #941 and boarded L.S.T. #696. I have been on many different L.S.T. ships in Europe and the Pacific, and I have to say that this latest craft is the worst. It is filthy, and the crew is not much better. I am thinking the invasion will be on May 5th.

<u>April 29, 1945</u>: The Japs hit us hard last night. They hit two ships in the harbor with torpedo bombs. I don't know how severe the damage was. We are now heading to our destination with the pontoons to make a causeway.

<u>May 6, 1945</u>: We stopped in the East Indies to rendezvous with other L.S.T.s who

have different types of pontoon gear. They have joined us on our voyage to Mankin. Before we left, I did have a chance to go ashore. I saw lots of WACS and nurses here who were mingling freely with officers. I saw a huge transport plane crash into a mountain and burst into flames. I hope there were not a lot of soldiers on it. I asked an Air Corpsman if there was a large number of infantry troops or Marines on the island. He said, "Yes, but they are all being used to keep the Japs in the hills." I thought maybe this would be the place that the invading force would use as a base of operations before the final push.

May 7, 1945: We left last night and are on our way to pick up troops for the invasion force. The invasion is scheduled to take place on May 16th. I just heard that Germany officially surrendered today. I think it is only a matter of time before the war is completely over. But the Japs are not going to surrender until they can't fight anymore.

<u>May 8, 1945</u>: Something is not right. My L.S.T. #696 is now alone, heading in the opposite direction of the rest of the convoy. Nobody is saying what the hell is going on. I hope they can get by without the pontoon pieces that we have.

<u>May 13, 1945</u>: We arrived in a new port yesterday, Morotai. Japanese-held islands are within sight, but a change of plans has taken place. We were underway to participate in the invasion. Now it is canceled or postponed.

Word is now we may go to Australia.

CHAPTER
TWENTY-FIVE

PREPARING FOR ANOTHER INVASION - BORNEO

<u>May 18, 1945</u>: We are still docked in Morotai. Destroyers have been shelling a Japanese-held island all day named Halmahara. It is 11 miles away, but it appears much closer. Apparently, 30,000 Japs are trapped on the island. They have not put up much anti-aircraft resistance, so American planes are using the island for bombing and strafing practice. It looks like the destroyers have hit something worthwhile because I can see a column of thick smoke rising over the

mountaintop in the distance. Those 30,000 human beings must have lost all hope when they look at all of the ships and planes that are coming to blast them and their brothers to kingdom come. As I write this, I can see the destroyers about five miles from me cruising back and forth. Just waiting for a sign of action from the Japs that will be their new target. As the battle goes on, I look at some of the troops around me. One is strumming a cowboy song on his battered guitar. Others are playing cards or shooting dice, seemingly unconscious of the action around them. After a while, the boom of guns became more or less commonplace.

A huge white hospital ship has just pulled out of port. I think it might be headed to Boreno to assist the invading force. The latest news (that is subject to change at a moment's notice) is that 350 Aussies [*Australian soldiers*] are to board with us. I have no idea where everyone will sleep when you add that number to the troops we already have. The invasion is to start on June 7th. We are to leave here on June 3rd. The 111th Battalion has been in two invasions to date. I have only received three letters in the past 80 days. I have written four short stories and 5,000 additional "circus words" [*Bob Behee was a circus performer before and after WWII*].

May 19, 1945: Tracers were shot into a nearby Jap island last night, so I didn't sleep. I wonder how much more I can take of this before I go completely bonkers. To make matters worse, we found out that the Ensign in charge forgot all of our medical records, so we had to take all of our shots and vaccinations again. That did not raise my spirits.

May 28, 1945: We now have the Aussies onboard. We are crowded, very crowded. Yet we still need to load more infantry soldiers in two days. They are saying that the D-Day for the invasion is now June 6th. D-Day on June 6th. Why does that date sound familiar? I'm sure I will be able to figure it out.

June 5, 1945: We are en route to Borneo. The minute we left this harbor behind, we were in Jap waters. One year ago, I was on my way to invade France today, and now I am getting ready for another D-Day in Borneo.

June 8, 1945: We picked up a Jap plane on radar, but thankfully he did not see us. We are in the enemy's "bowels" right now; anything can happen.

June 9, 1945: We are only a matter of miles off Borneo. There has been no sign of the Japs yet. It feels like a trap. It was damn hot today. This makes me even more irritable and uncomfortable. Many heavy ships have joined us. I don't have any fear whatsoever.

June 12, 1945: We pulled into the area at H-minus 3 [*3 hours before the invasion was to begin*]. We anchored and waited for the H-Hour tide. One Jap bomber came over and missed us by about 40 yards and was promptly shot down. Artillery from the destroyers, cruisers, and rocket gunboats opened up on the beach at 8:00 AM. Labuan

Island was our objective. It was only about four miles from Borneo. It had been mostly untouched except for the bombers that had attacked it today. The First Wave hit the beach at 9:00 AM and met with very slight resistance. They were able to walk to their first objective, the landing strip. It was then that the Japanese who had been hiding unloaded on them. They drove the troops all the way back to the beach. That is when our planes were called in to bomb and strafe, and the big guns on the ships opened up again.

We were slowly able to move inland again. Labuan Island is only about 35 miles. This makes it so that the Naval guns were able to surround the island and pound it mercilessly. The fighting on the island was still at a fresh pace. Fresh troops were added to the island at 10:00 AM to provide reinforcements for the First Wave. We seem to be making progress with Labuan Island. Enormous Borneo only seems like it is only yards away, but they have yet to get into the fight. The inactivity of the Japanese on Borneo is suspicious. We even caught three of their seaplanes on a beach that we were able to take out before they could get them in the air.

One type of airplane that Japs were able to get off the ground were their suicide bombers. The Japanese suicide dive bombers sure are a scary sight. They are being used so freely by the Japs that I felt certain they would strike my ship. Naturally, I felt they would miss me personally. I saw many German planes attacking our ships last year, but I never thought that a pilot would crash into a boat on purpose. The gunners all understand that they can't take their eyes off the sky for a second, or a plane might come crashing into their ship. It is hard to shoot down a plane that is flying right at you at high speed and is intent to crash into you.

June 13, 1945: After laying off the Labuan beach yesterday afternoon in broad daylight without being attacked, I think it is safe to say that the Japs are no longer a threat here. Word is that we will be leaving soon. Not sure if we are going to Morotai to plan for a new invasion of Southern Borneo or back to the Philippines to wait for who knows what. Wherever it is, I think we are leaving tomorrow in the L.S.T.

CHAPTER
TWENTY-SIX

HEADING BACK TO THE PHILIPPINES

June 14, 1945: We are back in a convoy heading North. This was the third invasion that the 111th Battalion had taken part in the Pacific. I heard some disturbing news from some of the troops who went ashore in Labuan. They said they saw bodies of the natives that the Japs had shot. There were a few natives who came out of hiding after the Japs had been defeated. They had the tendon cut on the back of their heel so they would not run away.

June 24, 1945: We are heading back to the Philippines. We are leaving today for

Tacloban again. There was a little bombing raid last night that was quite exciting while it lasted. We heard news from Labuan that the night after we pulled out, a bunch of Japs had snuck from Borneo and filtered through our lines. They attacked soldiers from the communications unit, killing 11 of them and cutting off their heads before escaping.

June 27, 1945: We are back in the Philippines. We should dock this evening. I see some ships shelling an island to the port side [*left side*]. No doubt it is part of a mopping-up operation. There are many aircraft carriers here. With their presence, it feels like a large operation in the North is imminent.

June 28, 1945: I have a better view of the massive amount of firepower that is anchored in Leyte Gulf. There are at least 12 aircraft carriers, along with a multitude of battleships, destroyers, heavy and light cruisers, and every other type of craft imaginable. This is the largest concentration of armed Naval power I have ever seen, and I was in on D-Day last year. No doubt, a terrific naval battle is being prepared for. I only wonder about the destination: Formosa, China, or Japan itself?

June 30, 1945: I am back in the camp on Calicoan in the Philippines. I am being told that we will stay here for a month and train for the invasion of Japan. Even though the Japanese islands have been bombed relentlessly for months, the Japanese have never surrendered in their long history.

They are preparing to fight to the death. It is estimated that hundreds of thousands of Allied soldiers might die trying to take the island. They would like us to train for the next month before the invasion.

CHAPTER
TWENTY-SEVEN

CLOSING STATEMENT FOR WWII

The month of July was mostly more of the same on Calicoan. We trained and endured heat and rain on a daily basis for about a month. At the end of July, my seabags were collected and stored. This brought back memories of storing my personal gear in England before heading to D-Day in France. I felt that the invasion of Japan was imminent, and I started to wonder if my luck would run out this time. But my luck held. On August 6th, we dropped the BIG bomb on Japan.

Then, on August 9th, we dropped another one. On September 2, 1945, World War II was over.

I never did see my sea bags again. I have no idea what happened to them. I returned to the States wearing my fatigues.

Here are all the places that I have traveled in the past two years: New York, Liverpool, Falmouth, Milford Haven, South Wales, Swansea, Southampton, Falmouth, Plymouth, Portland, Weymouth, Bayeux, Cherbourg, St. Lo, Boston, Norfork, Panama, Honolulu, Marshall Islands, Leyte, Calicoan, Samar, Tacloban, Hollandia, Los Negros, New Guinea, East Indies, Morotai, Labuan, Borneo, San Perdro, Chicago.

AFTERWORD "THE 111TH BATTALION USNCB"

In August of 1988, Robert G. Behee wrote a review for a book he had read on the unit he fought for in WWII, the 111th Battalion, otherwise known as the Fighting Seabees. In his review, he brought more detail to what he did with the Seabees in WWII. He seemed to think that history did not give the unit the respect it deserved.

The activities of the amphibious soldiers are not covered in this book [*he never says the name of the book*] in either name or action. I'll try to correct this.

Only the Americans had a unit like this to offload the L.S.T.s (landing craft tanks). The craft we used was called a "Rhino" for reasons I will never know. A Rhino Barge was made up of big pontoons, each measuring 6X8X4 feet. They were able to float in mere inches of water. These pontoons were loosely bolted together so that they had flexibility to slowly roll with the waves. A floating platform measured the pontoons 6 wide (48') by 10 pontoons long (80'). The center two forward pontoons held a ramp a foot wide for unloading vehicles onto the beach.

The Rhino was only one part of this vehicle. Its main propulsion was provided by a smaller, more powerful version of itself, which we called the "Tug." The Tug was 3 pontoons wide (24') by 5 pontoons long (40') and was driven by two large inboard engines that made it very agile and powerful. The purpose of the Tug was to pull the loaded Rhino to the beach.

How the entire process worked was an L.S.T. would travel as close as it could to the beach. Then, the Rhino and Tug would be unloaded, and thousands of pounds of men and material would be loaded onto the Rhino to be taken to the beach. When the Tug and Rhino approached the beach, the Tug would disengage, maneuver behind the Rhino, and push it onto shore. Once unloaded, the Tug would pull the Rhino off the beach and back to the waiting L.S.T.s for another load. So much for the make-up and activity of the Tugs and Rhino. Now, I will explain why they were needed.

Before D-Day, the Germans had implanted underwater obstacles all along the beaches we were going to invade. These obstacles consisted of railroad ties slanted seaward. They were about 7-8' high, at 10' intervals, for thousands of feet along the beaches. In some parts, they were five rows deep. These obstacles would tear out the bottom of any ship that tried to sail too close. But at high tide, the obstacles were underwater.

It was our job during the early part of the invasion to await high tide. Since our craft only drafted 11 inches, even when it was loaded, we were able to pass over the obstacles and land the cargo on the beach. Once ashore, if we were not able to unload in time, we would have to wait around until the next high tide. That was more than a little scary, as we were sitting ducks for being attacked.

At the time, in early 1944, the Rhino Barge was "hush, hush." The Allies did not want to give the Germans a clue what beaches we would be able to land on. We definitely did not want them to think we had craft that could make it over natural and man-made obstacles. So, we did all of our training and practicing tying up to the L.S.T.s in Wales, England.

Before the invasion, American, British, and Canadian ships were in large clusters in Plymouth Harbor. We saw Winston Churchill board selected British ships and share a tot of rum with the crew. American troops felt let down. We were given no ceremonial farewell or good luck shot of booze. We could have used a drink of grog, especially as the wind and seas began to rise.

We boarded our Tugs and Rhinos (they were now called our secret weapon) on the morning of June 4th to begin the D-Day invasion. We were dressed in full battle gear, with our duffle bags, so that we were ready for an extended stay on Omaha Beach. We were to stay on the beach until amphibious duties were completed. We would then take apart our disposable crafts to create pier docking facilities that would facilitate future unloading on the beach. That was if they were not able to capture some deepwater ports in France.

The Rhinos attached themselves to the L.S.T.s to cross the English Channel. These were the first ships, along with the battleships and destroyers, to sail for France. The sea was very rough, and the wind was blowing white caps off the waves. We were drenched on our open deck. The only cover we had was an open-ended pontoon that we used to house ammunition for our anti-aircraft gun. There were five of us on the Tug: two boatswain (of which I was one), gunner, signalman, and ensign. When we became too cold or wet, we took turns crawling on top of the ammunition for cover.

At 2:00 AM, we suddenly stopped forward progress to France. After sitting idle for a little while, we were ordered to return to the harbor. Later, we found out that the invasion had been postponed 24 hours.

The L.S.T. we were tethered to had sent a small boat to pick us up. This was a difficult task to accomplish in the dark in rough water. We were welcomed aboard warmly. Everyone was happy to see us because the rumor was that we had all been washed overboard. I was happy this was not the case. We got dry clothing, a meal, and some sleep before they deposited us back on the Rhino and Tug for another try.

The second departure was for real. Our participation in the D-Day invasion was not earth-shaking, but we did receive a Presidential Citation for our actions. The amazing thing was that out of the 1,200 men in our battalion, we only lost 120 men (10%). Before the battle, we were forecast to lose 780 men (65%). I was wounded while ashore after setting off a mine, but it was not enough to send me home.

EPILOGUE

By Robert G. Behee's grandson,
Robert Amich

In 1988, I followed in my Pawpaw's footsteps and joined the U.S. Navy. Many memories were shared as I stayed at my Pawpaw's Florida home in Sarasota during the hectic week leading up to the start of basic training in Orlando. My experience would be nothing compared to what he went through as he was heading off to war, but he still empathized with what I was about to go through.

In an amazing coincidence, I was stationed aboard the aircraft carrier USS George Washington, which would go on to serve as the centerpiece for the 50th Anniversary of the D-Day invasion in June of 1994. Unfortunately, my Pawpaw was not alive to share in the experience, but he was certainly with me in spirit. After a brief port call in Plymouth, England, the ceremonial armada sailed to Normandy and parked off-shore for the memorial activities. We then enjoyed a port call in Brest, France, that included a bus trip to Normandy with tours of the battle sites and cemeteries. I stood on Omaha Beach and honored my Pawpaw while I collected some sand and tried to imagine everything those brave soldiers and sailors endured.

Robert Amich at Omaha Beach

WWII VOCABULARY

5th Fleet Task Force: Established during World War II, the Fifth Fleet conducted extensive operations that led to the defeat of Japanese forces in the Central Pacific.

Barrage Balloons: An uncrewed tethered balloon used to defend ground targets against aircraft attack.

Beachmaster: A military officer in charge of the disembarkation phase of amphibious warfare.

Bean Counters: A bureaucrat perceived as placing excessive emphasis on controlling expenditure and budgets.

Blitz: An intensive or sudden military attack.

Bridge: Command center on a ship.

Booby Traps: A device or setup that is intended to kill, harm, or surprise a human.

C-Rations: Prepared, canned foods intended to be served when fresh food was unavailable.

Canteen: A place where sailors and soldiers could get food.

Cassino: A reference to a battle fought earlier in 1944 in Italy.

Chow: Slang term for food.

Coxswain: A Sailor in charge of navigating or steering a boat or ship.

DUCK: A six-wheel-drive amphibious craft used by the U.S. military during World War II.

E-Boats: Fast German Torpedo Boats.

Fighting French: Organized in London to fight for the liberation of France from German control and for the restoration of the republic.

Flak: The firing of guns from the ground at enemy aircraft.

Flying Bombs: An unmanned aerial vehicle or aircraft carrying a large explosive warhead.

Foxhole: A hole in the ground used by troops as a shelter against enemy fire.

Gabriel's Horn: Horn the archangel Gabriel blows to announce Judgment Day.

G.I. Joe's: Slang term for a WWII American infantry soldier.

Gold Braids: Slang term for Naval officers.

H-Hour: The time of day at which an attack, or military operation, is scheduled to begin.

Higgins Boat or L.C.V.P. *(landing craft, vehicle, personnel)*: A barge-like boat that could ferry 36 men to shore under fire.

Ice Boxes: An insulated cabinet with a compartment for ice used for cooling food.

Jap: A slang term for Japanese soldier or sailor.

Jerry/Jerries: A slang term for a German plane or soldier.

Jungle Jim: A popular 1948 American adventure film.

K-Rations: Three separately boxed meal units: breakfast, dinner, and supper.

King Neptune's Royal Order of the Shellbacks: An initiation rite commemorating a person's first crossing of the Equator.

L.C.A. *(Landing Craft Assault)*: Naval craft designed for conveying troops and equipment from a transport to a beach in an amphibious assault.

L.C.I. *(Landing Craft Infantry)*: An amphibious ship that could land 200 men on a beach.

L.C.M. *(Landing Craft Mechanized)*: A landing craft designed for carrying vehicles to the beach.

L.C.T *(Landing Craft Tanks)*: An amphibious assault craft for landing tanks on beachheads.

L.S.T. (*Landing Ship Tank*): Ship designed to transport and deploy troops, vehicles, and supplies onto foreign shores.

Liberty Ships: A cargo ship built in the United States during World War II.

Limey: A slang term for a British sailor or soldier.

Lord Haw-Haw: Nickname of William Joyce, who broadcast Nazi propaganda to the United Kingdom from Germany during WWII.

M.A.A. *(Masters at Arms)*: A naval petty officer appointed to carry out or supervise police duties on board a ship.

Machine Gun Pillbox: A type of blockhouse, or concrete dug-in guard-post, with machine guns.

Merchant Marines: Privately owned commercial ships of a nation that are not in the military.

M.P. *(Military Police)*: Responsible for police and disciplinary duties in an army.

Mines: Explosive device in the water to destroy submarines and surface vessels.

Minesweepers: A naval vessel used to clear an area of underwater mines.

M.I.A. *(Missing in Action)*: A member of the armed forces not yet confirmed as alive or dead.

Muster: Assemble (troops), especially for inspection or in preparation for battle.

Newsreels: A short film of news and current affairs made to be shown as part of the program in a movie theater.

Omaha Beach: D-Day landing in June 1944, part of the French coast where US troops landed.

P-38 Lightning: American single-seat, twin-piston-engine fighter aircraft.

Panzers: German word for tanks.

Platoon: The smallest military unit led by an officer, about 20-50 troops.

P.T. *(Patrol Torpedo Boat)*: A small fast patrol craft usually armed with torpedoes, machine guns, and depth charges.

Rommel: German General entrusted with the defense of France's coast against an Allied invasion.

SS *Eleazar Wheelock:* A ship that Bob was supposed to dock with.

Scuttled: To sink one's own ship by deliberately cutting a hole to let water in.

Scuttlebutt: Unconfirmed rumors from the battlefield.

Strafed: To rake ground troops with machine-gun fire from low-flying aircraft.

Tinsel strips: Thin strips of aluminum dropped from the air intended to blind or disrupt radar systems.

Tokyo Rose: Iva Toguri D'Aquino, an American woman, made propaganda radio broadcasts for the Japanese during the Second World War.

Utah Beach: A name given to the westernmost beaches where US troops landed on D-day in June 1944. There were fewer casualties here than at Omaha Beach.

WACS (*Women's Army Corps*): U.S. Army unit created during World War II to enable women to serve in noncombat positions.

War Bonds: Issued by a government to finance military operations in times of war without raising taxes.

Yellow Fever/Malaria: Tropical diseases spread by mosquitoes and caused flu-like symptoms.

PICTURES

Rhino Barge and Tug

L.S.T.

L.C.T.

L.C.V.P or Higgins Boat

DUKW or DUCK

German Artillery at Omaha Beach

Company C, Platoon 4

Bottom Row, left to right: K. F. Little, S2c; R. L. London, S1c; L. (n) Sanders, Jr., MM2c; R. J. Milligan, MMS2c; R. G. Behee, BM2c; K. O. Sargent, CM1c; W. F. Robertson, Cox; C. (n) Szymanski, MM3c; L. W. Sears, SF2c; A. R. Rybicki, S1c; F. L. Scaglione, S1c.

Middle Row, left to right: R. H. Swager, Jr., CM2c; W. R. Rhuda, CM3c; J. E. Roberson, S1c; W. H. Everett, Cox; V. (n) Brzostowski, S1c; S. V. De Augustino, CM3c; H. G. Hall, MM1c; R. A. Mur-

nane, S1c; L. M. Moore, S1c; J. W. Murray, S1c; D R. Mitton, S1c; R. C. Sanderson, S1c; R. A. Munich, S1c.

Top Row, left to right: M. L. Nuernberger, Lt. (jg); C. E. Schroeck, Cox; J. N. Cavanaugh, MoMM1c; A. B. Koziol, S2c; R. W. Mason, MM1c; D. N. Scara, S1c; C. O. Rawls, MoMM2c; H. F. Gilson, EM1c; R. R. Weeks, S1c; R. D. Roller, S2c; J. F. Roshone, S1c; J. F. Speer, CM1c; J. J. Lubecke, MM2c; R. (n) Mucci, S1c; W. E. Meadows, CSF.

Company C, Platoon 4 in the South Pacific

German Pillbox

Sept. 18th
STRIPES; Officers accomadations, well heated, furnished, radio,
and individual showers. Elite chow hall, bar and exquisite
officers club. Parties and weekly dances with nurses and wacs
very detrimental to the enlisted mens moral. Cold showers
were suggested for all hands. Lots of insubordination. Ridic-
ulous offer of Paris liberty to offset mens resemblance of
parties. Officers had official liberty since Cherbourg was
taken. Man busted up in auto wreck is now laying in the hospital. No attempt has been made to Xray. The same is the case
of a mashed arm. The doctor said, "If we get up to Cherbourg,
I'll have it Xrayed." He's been suffering for two weeks and
still no picture.

By October, 1944 most of the 11th Batt.
had been shipped back to the "States".
"B" company - who had been manning the
rhines in France. Were sent back to
England. Leave was proposed and I
had gone so far as to making arrangements
to visit the "Millers" in Scotland.
Then came the "Battle of the Bulge).
All leaves cancelled. We remained in
this state until we were shipped back
to the States - on a stormy sea.
My ear healed - killing any chance
of a medical discharge.
I was given a 30 day leave -
then shipped to the South Pacific -
thru the Panama Canal. Still
with the 111th CB's.

Bob's Handwritten Diary Entry.

Omaha Beach, June 1944

PICTURE CITATIONS

A Crusader I tank emerges from the tank landing craft TLC-124. 26 Apr. 1942. Https:// En.Wikipedia.Org/Wiki/Landing_craft_tank.

A DUKW in use by American troops in France. DUKW.Image2.Army.jpg.

The Higgins Boat – 9 Things You Might Not Know About the Landing Craft That Changed History. 6 June 1944. WikiCommons.

LST (MK2) Class Tank Landing Ships-Allied Warships of WWII. June 1944. Uboat.Net.

Rhino ferry RHF-3 approaches Normandy beaches 6 June 1944.jpg. 6 June 1944.

BONUS STORY

YOU'RE IN THE NAVY NOW!

By Robert G. Behee

Editor's Note: This is a humorous semi-autobiographical account of Bob Behee's introduction to the United States Navy. In this narrative account, Bob refers to himself as "Denning."

War had been declared! The fact that it had been declared over a year ago meant little for two young men about to embark on an adventure. War had been declared, and Hal and I wanted to fight. Once we made this decision, there was to be no turning back. We walked into the recruiting office. A bright and cheerful building made up like the Fourth of July (the building was made up, not us), knowing we would be changed men when we left.

"Where do we sign up?" Hal asked the first man in uniform we saw. As he looked at us, a little smile began to play at the edges of his mouth. Much like a man just about ready to set the hook on a fish that had been nibbling on his bait. I assumed he was a colonel because he had two stripes on his sleeve.

"What branch do you want, buddy? Army?" He looked at us with a gleam in his eye.

"Oh, I don't know." Hal drawled, trying to look coy and hide his naivety. "What branches have you got?"

The "colonel" gave us a look that was somewhere between excitement and exasperation and he began to recite from a script in his head.

"Well, there's the Army, Navy, and Marines. Each of these branches has an Air Corps branch within them. Then you can break it down further to Intelligence, Engineers, Amphibious, Submarines, and Seabees, to name a few."

I was overwhelmed and just stared at the man like a walleyed pike, but Hal spoke up with his usual wit and charm. "Seabees, what is that, a new breakfast cereal?"

The "colonel" had now officially had enough of our stupidity. He spoke to us in a slow, measured tone. "Seabees are the army engineers' equivalent in the navy. It is a new outfit."

"Which unit will get us into action the soonest?" I asked.

I did not understand what the "colonel" was talking about, but I felt I had to break my silence so that he would know I could speak.

The man was now done with us. "I'm sorry, fellows, but you are going to have to ask someone else. My job is to guard this door, not campaign for volunteers."

"What are you guarding against?" Hal asked the man.

"Guarding against?" The "colonel" repeatedly looked at Hal like he was the dumbest person he ever saw. "Why, the enemy, of course!"

Hal was not yet done. "Has the enemy ever tried to enlist in our armed forces?"

"Well, I imagine that it has been done." The man said with a puzzled look on his face.

I felt it was my turn to speak up. "Tell me, guard, how do you tell who the enemy is when he comes to the door? Does he speak Japanese or wear a swastika on his arm?"

We beat a hasty retreat up the stairs, leaving the guard sputtering like a fuse, yelling about smart-assed kids wasting his time.

Hal and I walked into the first office we found at the top of the stairs. When we opened the door, we saw a large room that housed many desks. These desks were all manned by serious countenanced officers. We walked smartly to the first desk and I noticed a huge banner that was hung on the wall behind it. It had a crossed anchor pattern with rope all tangled up in it. In large letters on top of the anchors was the word "NAVY." Beneath this banner was a captain sitting at a desk. I thought the man was a captain because he had two bars on his collar, and I knew they did not just give those bars away for nothing.

I started talking before Hal could open his mouth. "Captain, which branch of the service will get us into action the fastest?"

He looked up from the desk with a pained expression. "I'm no 'Captain,' Son." He spoke slowly, like he was talking to a child. I'm a Lieutenant; in the Navy, an Army Captain Insignia signifies a Lieutenant."

"What is an Army Lieutenant in the Navy?" I asked out of curiosity.

The man took a deep sigh and said, "A Second Lieutenant in the Army is called an Ensign in the Navy, and a First Lieutenant in the Army is called a Lieutenant Junior Grade in the Navy." Then his mood changed, and he began to tell Hal and me about the wonders of the United States Navy.

Then he looked at me and said something that would have a profound effect on my life: "In answer to your original question, the branch that will get you overseas the fastest is the Seabees."

"Huh!" Hal scoffed. "Breakfast food again."

The lieutenant continued talking without even addressing Hal's strange comment. "They want men of skilled labor. Your training is shortened based on how many years of experience you already have in a trade. This experience is enough for the job, and your combat training is only limited to emergency defense."

Hal spoke next. "How long will it take for us to get overseas?" He was anxious to get into the thick of things.

The lieutenant smiled and said, "It's possible that you would be en route to a foreign theater of operation three months after you start training."

Hal looked over at me, but my attention was riveted on a pretty blonde calmly walking on the street below us, unaware of the momentous decision about to occur in the office two stories above her.

"It's done!" Hal exclaimed. "Where do we sign up?" he asked, volunteering my life without consulting me.

It was the lieutenant who put the brakes on. "I don't handle enlistments for that branch. You need to see Captain Jardine on the fifth floor."

We did not even say "goodbye" to the lieutenant. Hal grabbed me by the arm and practically sprinted for the elevator.

Now was my chance to take a step back and become the voice of reason. "Not so fast, Hal!" We had stopped in the hall in front of the elevator. "Let us not hurry into this thing. We really don't know what this Seabee thing is all about. Let's go out and have a drink and talk this over."

I thought the mention of a drink would get him out of the building. I wanted to get him some fresh air. He really needed it!

"I will get a drink after I commit to defending this country that I love."

His glassy-eyed patriotism was almost scary. The reflection of Old Glory was so plainly etched in his eyes that his eyeballs seemed to ruffle like little flags. I knew there was no direction to go but up to the fifth floor.

We stepped into the waiting elevator, and Hal breathlessly gave our destination to the solemn-looking elevator operator.

"Welcome aboard, boys, welcome aboard." The man said in a monotone voice without changing his expression. "Flooooor?"

It was eerie how he asked the question. I began to wonder again whether we were doing the right thing. Before I could say anything, Hal told the man to take us to the fifth floor. After an eternity, the elevator stopped, and "Sir-Happiness" opened the door slowly. He eyed Hal and me strangely as we disembarked. I swear I heard a shrill, hysterical laugh as the doors closed and he headed down.

Before long, Hal and I found ourselves in front of another officer.

I thought he was a corporal this time because he had a little eagle on his collar, but I did not want to get caught up in another string of confusing rank fire, so I said, "Good morning, Captain." That seemed to please him because he smiled.

"I'm not a captain," he corrected, "I'm Colonel Rigby. I am here to see the captain myself."

I could have left well enough alone, but I had to open my big mouth. "Oh, you're a colonel. I thought you were a corporal. I always get those two mixed up." At this point, the smile left the man's face. I hastened to cover up my blunder, but I only dug myself in deeper. "I didn't think you were a captain. I only called you that because the captain, I mean the Navy lieutenant downstairs, told me to come and see a Navy captain up here."

The colonel looked at me and gave me a wicked smile because he knew just how much fun bootcamp would be for me. However, since I was still a civilian, I was untouchable for the time being. I had no sooner got the colonel-corporal thing straightened out when I walked into another man who I assumed had to be another colonel.

"Good morning, Captain." Colonel Rigby said as he stood up.

I had enough of craziness. It was too much for me, so I got up and started for the stairs. At this point, Hal snapped out of the "Stars and Stripes Forever" march that was playing on an endless loop in his head, and he grabbed me by my arm and twisted it a little bit. I stayed. Colonel Rigby did not linger long. He talked to the other man about recruit shortages, then left and went on his way. He did not look at me as he turned to go.

The colonel-captain, an officer of some kind, beckoned Hal and me to come into his room. We went obediently. Hal sat down and put one of his legs over the corner of the man's desk. I knew this was not very proper, so I sat while resting both elbows on the desk and cradling my chin in my hands.

The captain frowned, looked at the recruitment goal report on his desk, and sighed deeply. Then he cleared his throat and purred. "So, you boys want to join the Seabees?"

I settled for a slight nod while Hal exclaimed, "Yeah!" Then he went into a song and dance about wanting overseas duty pronto so he could stick it to the Axis.

The captain let him run off at the mouth for a minute; then he asked what skills we had and what our trades were. Hal exclaimed he was a body-and-fender man at the present. Then he proceeded to list more jobs he had done since he was ten years old. I thought I would take a more conservative route and only tell him about one job.

I said with no hesitation. "I am a rigger captain with 15 years of experience." (A rigger is anyone who attaches or detaches lifting equipment for loads or lifting devices).

"How old are you now?" The captain asked in a skeptical tone.

"Twenty-four, Sir," I confessed.

The captain's eyebrows rose. He was no doubt marveling at my being a rigger at the tender age of nine. He shook his head a little and continued.

"I'll tell you what to do, men. Get two letters of recommendation from your former employers and bring them to me. I will then see about getting you a specialist rating."

He began explaining the benefits that being a specialist would grant us, but Hal didn't care to stick around. He was truly on a mission, dragging me along with him.

"Okay," Hal said while sliding his foot off the captain's desk, knocking over his wastebasket and strewing scraps of paper all over the floor. "We'll be back tomorrow with the letters."

As Hal and I left the room to attend to our tasks, I took one last look at the captain. From the look on his face as he surveyed the garbage on his floor, I could not tell if he thought Hal was issuing a promise or a threat.

The next morning, Hal was waiting for me as I dismounted from the streetcar. The

Loop was teeming with traffic, and we had to push our way along the sidewalk.

"What kept you so long?" Hal asked with an air of impatience.

"I didn't like one of the letters of recommendation I got, so I rewrote it," I replied.

There was a long line of serious-faced youths lined up in front of the recruiting station. Hal and I had an appointment, so we pushed our way through the crowd to the front of the line and met face-to-face with the guard. Before he could say anything to us, I spoke up.

"Good morning, Corporal." I made sure to emphasize his rank so he knew that I (and everybody behind me) knew he was not a colonel. The guard just scowled at me, but if looks could kill, I would have dropped dead. This service life was nuts, but I was learning fast.

Hal didn't feel like waiting for the elevator, so we raced up the stairs to the captain's office. The good captain looked at our letters intently. After several minutes of silence, he spoke to Hal.

"Darling," that was Hal's last name. "With your skills, I'm going to make you a rolly-motor-macaroni first class." At least, that is what his new title sounded like to me. "There are lots of chances for advancement in the ship-fitters class." Hal had no idea what he would be doing for the next few years of his life, but he stood there beaming with pride.

"Denning, (that's me) you'll qualify as a Coxswain." (the person in charge of a boat, particularly its navigation and steering).

Oh boy, I thought, a coxswain! I could not believe my luck. I agreed readily. Anxious but incredibly happy (I was so naïve). I sat back and did a mental search for the place of coxswain within the ladder of ranks.

Yesterday, I learned that a captain was above two kinds of lieutenant. I knew there was something between them, though. A rank that was equal to a major or a second lieutenant in the Army. My heart beat rapidly; could that be a coxswain? I was ready to tell the captain that I thought the rank a bit more than I could handle, but then I thought better of it. "After all, the captain knows what he is doing," I argued inwardly, "Besides, I am a pretty good rigger. What do you know, a coxswain! Wait until I tell my wife."

The good captain handed us cards to sign and told us to report immediately to the third floor for a physical examination. I thought his voice sounded a little loud and sharp, but I was too elated at my good fortune to speak to him about it then.

Hal and I scampered down the stairs like children at play. It felt like every second we delayed, we were depriving our valuable services to Uncle Sam. When I opened the door marked "Physical Examinations" and stepped inside, I knew there would be no turning back for me.

The physical exam was a joke of the most impersonal nature; our eyes were checked (two, okay next), limbs counted (four), and a blood test taken. Hal was particularly squeamish about having a needle stuck in his arm. As we stood in line, a teenager younger than me looked at Hal and could tell that Hal needed some encouragement.

"Nothing to it, fellows," he boasted. "I've had this done hundreds of times, and I tell you, you won't feel a thing." Then he proceeded to flex his muscles for us, make a few obscene sexual remarks, and generally make a pest of himself. I noticed the corpsman with the big needle eye up the braggart and gave a big smile.

When the boy got before the corpsman, he continued his act of braggadocio. With both of his arms bared, he said, "Take your pick, Doc, look no blindfold." He grinned at Hal and me as if he had made a funny remark. I felt sorry for him at this point.

The smile was gone from the corpsman's face. It was replaced by the frown of a determined needle pusher. I knew this man was going to give the plunge of his needle all the skill and experience that his years of flesh pricking had given to him. The corpsman grasped the youth firmly by the elbow, bringing the softer, whiter under-part of the boy's arm into view. He looked directly into the boy's eyes and then plunged his needle into the boy's soft flesh. Parry, thrust! The needle pierced the vein and passed through it, causing a large bruise and a great deal of pain. The man said, "Oops," and quickly withdrew the needle to try again. The second attempt brought the same results as the first. Perspiration began to form on the boy's brow.

He did not look as tough as he did a few minutes before. Lucky for him, the third time was the charm. The corpsman looked up at the boy with a smile of triumph on his lips, and then he grasped the plunger and slowly drew blood from the vein.

When finished, he looked at the boy again and said, "Put this bandage on your arm and keep it bent double." Then he added, "Perhaps you better stand by the open window to get some air." Then, with a relenting, sympathetic smile on his lips, he got up to help the pasty-faced boy towards the window.

By then, the boy had regained some of his former swagger and jerked free. "I don't need any air. I feel great!" He turned around to face us and said, "What did I tell you? No sweat." Then, he staggered across the room and fell to the floor before he reached the door. In all of the commotion, I looked at Hal and found he had fainted before the corpsman had even touched him with a needle.

As they wheeled Hal to the sick ward, my time had arrived to meet the needle. Maybe the corpsman felt a little guilty about what he had done to the boy because he seemed to take his time and stick me right the first time he tried. With Hal down for the count (at least for the next few hours), I had to continue by myself.

I was given my first touch of regimentation a short while after the physical examination. Chits were issued to each of us, and we were told to fall into columns of threes in front of the recruiting station. We went outside (about 40 guys) and formed columns, files, horizontals, and verticals. It was the first time I ever saw a "Q" formation. A fellow with a lot of stripes on his arm came out and did a lot of loud cursing when he saw us screwing around. He put us in three long lines of equal numbers and walked us down the sidewalk. As we passed women walking down the street, cat calls, wolf whistles, and hyena laughter could be heard from the ranks. Yes, we had the makings of fine-fighting men.

We stopped at a cafeteria and filed in.

Crowding and pushing for places at the front of the line started immediately. After some doing, I found a tray and was shoved along the assembly line. I was only able to get a lick and smell of several "food-like" items. It did not matter because I was not hungry anyway. I was, however, thoroughly disgusted with the actions of my selfish, greedy fellow soldiers.

After lunch, I returned with the men back to the station and checked on Hal. He was still sick from the blood test, so I had to proceed alone.

The men assembled were given cards of acceptance by the Seabees and told to report to the draft board and have their names removed from their list of draftees. A man in charge called our names and handed me a list. Lo and behold! I had been chosen to lead this group. I faltered for a moment, then remembered I now bore the noble rank of coxswain. I was now a leader of men.

Squaring my shoulders, I stood up straight, looked into the man's bloodshot eyes, and shouted, "Yes, Sir!"

I was issued streetcar tickets and told where the chartered car would be waiting to take us the six blocks to the medical examination building. As the men swarmed into the streetcar, I gave the conductor a stack of tickets. It was then that I gave my first order. "You may smoke them if you have them, men." The conductor gave me a strange look and continued counting the tickets. He then counted the men and informed me that I was two fares short. I had to shell out the additional money from my own pocket. Being in charge had its pluses and minuses.

When we arrived at the medical examination building, we were given a REAL physical examination. This examination was no joke. It was complete and embarrassing.

We were stripped of all our clothing and covered in iodine. After coughing out either side of our mouths, we had to stand and touch the floor with our fingertips. This was done both with and without the doctor doing some touching of his own. This assembly line of flesh moved quickly from room to room, passing probing fingers and prying eyes until we came to another blood test.

It was here that I ran into Hal again. He was passed out cold and had upset a hundred naked men as he was being revived from his latest bloodletting experience. I waited as he was brought back to consciousness, and we finished the physical quiz together.

The last doctor we visited relieved the tension and strain of the morning. I learned later that he was a psychoanalyst. I entered his cubby hole of an office, and he took advantage of me right away. He placed me where the sun was shining in my face and told me to "relax and compose myself." Just imagine me in the nude, sitting on a cold chair, with the sun blinding me. Relaxing was the farthest thing from my mind. I did not know if this guy was going to crown me with a mallet, stick another needle in me, or explore the inner recesses of my body. I squinted so I could see him better. I wanted to be prepared for whatever was coming next. This man reminded me of a Cyclops. He had glasses with tremendously thick lenses that magnified his bulging eyes. He stared at me unblinkingly.

"Do you like girls?" He shot the question at me suddenly. I thought this was the stupidest question that anyone had ever asked me. Because he was so loud and obnoxious, I replied.

"No, I'm queer for rice pudding." I must have said what he wanted to hear because he dismissed me without further questioning.

Hal told me he enjoyed his questioning even more. His doctor used the "smiling approach." He would ask frivolous questions in the mildest, happy tone. Then jump up and shout some crazy damned thing.

"He seemed very nervous," Hal said. "It must be his job."

There we were, fully clothed once again, awaiting the results of the most grueling and thorough physical examination ever conceived by man. Maybe that's a bit strong, but it was much more than just counting limbs and digits.

We were all seated in a large hall and waited for our names to be called. Hal and I were discussing our respective fates when a Lieutenant from the Army Air Corps appeared from the back of the hall. He went down the rows and softly inquired,

"Any of you men want to join the Air Corps?"

If anyone acted interested, he would set them aside and give a great sales pitch that he had practiced before. He was able to "Shanghai" several men from the hall. If I had any interest in joining, I soon found out that I was overage for anything but ground crew.

Once again, I was able to hold my tongue—no need to start throwing my rank around before I got my uniform on.

Hal and I passed the physical. We were given our records and told to report back to the recruiting office. There, we were fed a box lunch (Uncle Sam paid no expense) and waited around for a few hours. A deck of cards magically appeared, and a poker game commenced to idle away the time. A Chief Petty Officer came over to politely tell us that gambling was frowned upon in the Navy. We frowned at him and continued to play. Unable to break up the game, he asked us to kindly keep our coins off the table and out of sight. We kept our money in our hands and used a hat to place our bets. I lost.

An officer finally came into the room and herded us into an alcove (some 50 of us) and placed us in an assemblage of formation. The officer rattled off a stereotyped speech of what we were about to do. He had us raise our right hand and repeat after him, which we all did. Then he said, "Congratulations, Sailors!" Yippee, we were in the Navy!

It reminded me somewhat of my marriage. In typical movie fashion, we waited until the last minute and caught the judge just as he was leaving his office to catch a train.

Then, after the hastiest ceremony in history, he said these immortal words, "It's too late to change your minds now."

Maybe those words are what the Navy officer should have closed with because, brother, we were in it for the duration and then some! We had a bit more waiting to do after the officer shook hands with everybody. A yeoman made out leave papers for those who wanted their last seven days of freedom before turning in for duty.

While we waited, the deck of cards appeared and I wanted to see if I could win back my money. The cards had not even been dealt when the same chief from before came storming over to us and barked,

"Put that deck away! Now!" Then he looked my way and pointed at me.

"You, grab a broom and sweep up in here!" He didn't have to be trite and remind me, "You're in the Navy now!" I knew it.

Hal and I decided to be stupid again and waive our leave. "We're on active duty now," we said proudly. We were then told to stand by. That meant more hours of waiting (without cards). At supper time, when I was the hungriest, weariest, and most disgusted, we were finally called up to the desk and told.

"I'm giving you men overnight liberty."

Freedom for the night. What happy words these were.

"Report back here at 08:00 (pronounced oh-eight-hundred). Bring with you only the barest of necessities. The Navy furnishes everything for you."

I was happy to get out of there but worried about the time thing all the way home. I could not remember if you added twelve to that and then divided the balance or took the square root. Ah, hell. I felt like a four-year-old because I did not know what time it was.

My wife was surprised to see me walk in. She figured I would be on my way overseas. She had already given my shirts to a neighbor and cleaned out my drawers. I went to my neighbor to get one of my shirts to wear. I was questioned at great length as I wolfed down a hastily prepared meal. When I mentioned that I had to report back at oh-eight-hundred tomorrow, my wife showed some sympathy and said, "You'll have to get up early to make it by eight o'clock."

"Eight o'clock!" I shouted inwardly. That was it. You needed to subtract the zero.

"Oh-eight-hundred," I corrected her. "Please wake me at oh-five-hundred." Boy, was I turning into an old salt.

My wife wanted to pack an old sea chest full for me, but I knew better.

"I'll send for it later, honey. Just pack the small wardrobe trunk for me."

It was not necessary to awaken me at 05:00. I was already awake at 03:00, 02:00, 01:00, and 00:00. After a large breakfast and a few fond farewells, my baby trunk and I were off.

I met Hal outside the recruiting office.

We entered the building and reported to the chief. He told us to be seated and wait until he called us. He eyed my luggage and asked what it was. When I responded that it was my personal gear, he shook his head sadly with a pained look on his face. Later, I noticed the yeomen muttering among themselves while glancing at me and snickering.

"Just jealous of my higher rank," I mumbled to Hal.

We sat idle all day, except to be led like children to a nearby restaurant to be fed. When we got back, they were shutting down the place. The chief's eyes fell on us, and we were called before the desk.

"Darling-Denning, I'm giving you another overnight pass. You will return at 08:00."

We thanked him and headed for the door. "Denning!" The chief barked, "You better see if you can't get your personal gear in a smaller bag. Just bring a toothbrush, razor, toothpaste, two pairs of socks and underwear. Only enough to last a few days. Remember, the Navy furnishes everything."

When I arrived home this time, my wife acted like I was a slacker who was going AWOL. Before she turned me in as a traitor, I convinced her I had no idea what was causing the delay. I was too angry at the Navy to eat, so I just said, "Wake me at five o'clock. To hell with that 05:00 crap." Then I stomped off to bed.

Back at the recruiting station the following morning, I asked the chief what the delay was.

"You don't ask questions," he stormed at me. "You just do as you're told."

As I walked meekly back to my chair, Hal stuck his tongue at the chief (when he had turned his back). More men than usual came in and joined us today. When I questioned them quietly so the chief couldn't hear, they told me they had completed their seven days of leave and were all reporting back for duty.

Before we knew what was happening, we were on a train. After many hours, we arrived in Williamsburg, Virginia. A hot and dirty group of men disembarked at the station. A sailor with a voice of authority was there to greet us.

"Alright, you guys, line up over here!" "Over here" was smack dab in the hottest, sunniest spot for miles around. "Who's got the muster," he shouted.

A chief in a shining new uniform handed him a sheet. I discovered that the chief was going to Williamsburg for the same reason we were: boot camp. Where he got the rating and uniform is another story. I realized that my rating had been overlooked.

After the muster had been called and we had everyone accounted for, a group of open trucks pulled up. A man yelled, "Get in the trucks, and I will take you for some good old Navy chow."

There was a mad dash to the trucks.

Shoving and pushing seemed to be the order of the day. Hal and I had to crawl over men hanging on the tailgate. We begged our pardon and got scowls in return. Then we were off to Camp Perry. We passed herds of men fenced in along the way. We noticed that many men were clinging to the fences near the road. As they saw us pass by, a large chant began to echo in our heads.

"You'll be Sorrrrrrrrrrrrrrryyyyyyyy."

We went onward until we arrived at a place with the highest fence I had ever seen. This was to be our first stop on our mass conversion of turning from civilians to fighting men. Again, we were lined up and mustered, but this time, the sailor was more humane and had us stand under a roof. Not a room, just a roof supported by four poles. This would have been great earlier in the day, but now the sun was lower and shined directly into our perspiring faces. I realized the sailor had been talking for some time, so I thought I should listen.

"…and if you have any cameras, knives, straight razors, you will turn them in now, and they will be sent home for you. Any man withholding such items from this point will be placed on report and disciplined."

He split us alphabetically into groups of 20, and then an aide took charge. He walked us to a nearby barracks and told us to grab a bunk. We had no sooner set our bags down and laid back on the slightly soiled mattress when we heard the words "Chow time!"

We staggered out the door without washing and started the hike to the mess hall.

We walked out of the gate, down a dusty road, over a hill and dale (we even forded a creek). Onward, forever onward, we finally were at "Ye Old Mess Hall." I was starving after my long journey. When I looked around at hundreds of sweaty and smelly men, I lost my appetite. We picked up hot trays and timidly inspected their cleanliness as men yelled.

"Keep the line moving!" This was not an order or a command. It sounded like (and probably was) a threat. We extended our trays to the men serving food out of gigantic pans. It was clear by the gleam in the server's eyes that they knew we were novices.

"Straighten out that tray, no turn it around!"

They would yell as they dropped a serving of piping hot mashed potatoes on your overlapping thumb. I discovered that some of those boys were splendid shots. They could even get you when you carried your hand completely beneath the tray.

Most of us had never seen so much food served in such large quantities, so we lagged as we ogled the serving line.

"Keep moving, Bud! Let's Go! Move it!" The entire line would shout.

We were still wearing our civilian clothes, so the men took out their frustration and the pain they had accumulated over the past weeks of boot camp on us.

We wandered away from the line with our heavily laden trays. I could not see any place to sit at one of the long tables filled with sailors. More experienced men in this "survival of the fittest" format would brush past us to take seats that materialized out of nowhere. I finally found a seat against the wall. I dripped gravy on a few men as I pushed through the narrow aisle, my head held high over their heads. After a few scowls and curse words, I sat down to eat.

I noticed perspiration from my brow was dripping onto my food. It was made worse when I observed there were still puddles of former diners' perspiration slopped all over the table. The final straw was when I attempted to drink the green, warm, and tasteless liquid that had been splashed into my cup and found I could barely get it down. It was then I discovered I was not hungry. I grabbed my tray and headed for the nearest garbage can. I prayed that I would not throw up or pass out until I got outside.

Once outside, all I wanted to do was find our guide and trudge back to the barracks. My luck then changed, and I found Hal. He was also lost.

"Let's try to find our way back alone," I suggested.

"To Chicago?" Hal questioned hopefully. "No, to our area," I said as I began to walk.

"Oh no! Not me," Hal said worriedly. "I'm not going into that swampy jungle without a guide."

"Cloe!" Hal called out when he saw our guide, whose name was actually Jack.

"Didn't take you fellows long to eat; no one else is even finished yet," he said.

I eyed Hal and said, "You too?" He nodded back, and we both wondered if we would eat again.

Our little group finally formed, and we all marched back to the barracks and got ready for bed.

"Hit the sack early, men," Jack said. "You're going to have a busy day tomorrow."

At 05:00, a bugle sounded, disturbing my dreams from home. Instantly, the lights flooded on as men began to fall out of their bunks. This was serious business.

"Hit the deck!" Jack yelled. "Lots to do this morning. Rise and shine!" He went around the bunks, shaking those who seemed reluctant to move.

After another endless hike to the mess hall, I almost ate my breakfast. It was time for another physical. This time, when we were stripped of our clothes, they were put in a box to be shipped home. This was our last touch of civilian life. It was a sad parting. Upon completing another rather thorough physical, we were given what the Navy provided. They issued each of us a set of underwear, socks, G.I. shoes, a pair of blue denim pants, and a blue shirt. In a matter of minutes, the clothes were sticking to my body in the damp heat. We were then herded into a room with a multitude of desks.

"Sit down!" I was told, and then the interrogation began. "Name, age, former occupation, do you play a musical instrument, what sports do you like, any hobbies?"

I was all set for him to ask me if I liked girls again.

"That's all here. Go to the allotment department. Next!" I got up and left.

"Married, wife's name?" Here they went again with the questions. "Do you care to add to the usual allotment?"

I hesitated and tried to figure out what he was talking about. He noticed my confusion and continued.

"I see by the records that your base pay is $78.00 a month."

"$78.00 a month!" I interrupted. "But there must be some mistake. I'm a coxswain!"

"Yes." He spoke slower, as if he were talking to a child. "A coxswain is a Third-Class Petty officer."

"Petty!" I shouted. "Why, I am a rigger!" I said with the air of a wounded aristocrat.

He shook his head and continued. "A base pay of $78.00, with $22.00 deducted for an allotment, will leave you with $56.00 per month." This man was truly a math genius.

"No, I don't want to increase my allotment at this time." I was stunned. My rank had been snatched from me without a word.

"Insurance department next," he pointed to a desk a few rows over.

"It is the duty of all men going into the service…"

I wasn't interested in listening to this man's sales pitch. I was a third-class petty officer. Hal even outranked me with his first class, and he was my junior in age.

"Well, what will it be, sailor?" The insurance man asked with a smile. "Do you want the entire $7.00 per month deduction?"

"Yeah, give me the works," I said without much thought.

That was it. Until I saw that $7.00 was taken off each check, which only left me with $49.00 a month. That would have still been OK, but I must have accidentally agreed to increase my allotment or bought war bonds because when I arrived overseas a few months later, I was only taking home $28.00 a month. Some two years later, I was still only making $28.00, even though, at that point, I was a Boatswain Mate First-Class.

During my time in WWII, I saw combat in England, France, the Philippines, and Borneo. However, it was not until 1945 that I finally caught up to Hal's First-Class rating. Unfortunately, by then, Hal was no longer with me, or with anyone for that matter. Unless you want to consider him being with his maker.

BIOGRAPHY

ROBERT (BOB) G. BEHEE

Robert (Bob) G. Behee was born on October 10, 1916, in Kansas City, Missouri. He was born into the circus. His mother, Leta Hewitt Behee, was a bareback rider, and his father, Earl Behee, was a single trapeze artist. Bob was an acrobat and an aerialist in many circuses, including the Alexander Teeterboard Troupe, which he joined when he was 12.

He met his wife, Margaret "Mickey" Miller, in the circus. They were both performing in Indianapolis, Indiana. Mickey was in a vaudeville dancing act.

Bob joined his brother Clayton and sister-in-law, Rose, as a catcher, performing in "The Flying Behees." For many years, they worked at the prestigious Shrine Circus and other leading circuses, including the Ringling Bros. and Barnum & Bailey Circus.

In December 1941, the Behees were working in Honolulu and housed in the Schofield Army barracks when the Japanese planes drone over the island on the morning of December 7.

Bob enlisted as a Navy Seabee when he was 27 years old.

He kept a war diary as he prepared for and experienced the invasion of Normandy on D-Day at Omaha Beach. He later received a Purple Heart for his injuries. He continued his service in the South Pacific.

After his service, he returned to the circus. Bob's circus acts were featured in several national magazines, including *Newsweek*, where he was pictured on the cover of the May 19, 1947 issue with "The Flying Behees." He was also in National Geographic in March 1948.

In 1950, "The Flying Behees" performed in Australia for two years.

After the circus, Bob went to school and received a degree in electronics from the American Television Institute of Technology in Chicago. He then settled in Milwaukee, Wisconsin, with his family.

Bob lived with his wife, Mickey, and daughter, Bonnie, for nearly 20 years in Milwaukee, where he was assistant chief engineer at WITI-TV (Channel 6). Bob and Mickey moved to Sarasota, Florida, in 1971, where he helped found the city's first local television station, WXLT, where he was chief engineer and production engineer.

Moving to Sarasota was like going home for Bob and Mickey because it was the headquarters and winter home of the Ringling Bros. and Barnum & Bailey Circus. They enjoyed going to the "Showfolks of Sarasota" to visit with their circus friends.

In 1990, Bob and Mickey returned to Wisconsin to celebrate their 50th wedding anniversary with their daughter, Bonnie Behee-Semler, and family and friends.

Bob passed away on September 27, 1991, after a battle with cancer.